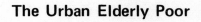

The Urban Elderly Poor

The Urban Elderly Poor

Racial and Bureaucratic Conflict

Richard S. Sterne
University of Akron

James E. Phillips
Aging Project

Alvin Rabushka
University of Rochester

Lexington Books
D. C. Heath and Company
Lexington, Massachusetts
Toronto   London

Library of Congress Cataloging in Publication Data

Sterne, Richard S.
  The urban elderly poor.

  Bibliography: p. 137
  1. Aged—Rochester, N.Y. 2. Poor—Rochester, N.Y. 3. Rochester,
N.Y.—Race question.
I. Phillips, James E., joint author. II. Rabushka, Alvin, joint author.
III. Title.
HV4046.R6S7   362.6'042'0974789   73-18014
IBSN 0-669-91835-0

Published simultaneously in Canada.

Printed in the United States of America.

International Standard Book Number: 0-669-91835-0

Library of Congress Catalog Card Number: 73-18014

Contents

List of Figures

List of Tables

Preface

This book critically evaluates whether programs designed to help the poor help themselves are meaningful. In a report published for the Special Committee on Aging of the United States Senate, John B. Martin, Commissioner of the Administration on Aging, asserted in 1971 that the Model Cities Program has the potential for significantly improving the lives of the elderly, who constitute a disproportionately high percentage of the population in the central cities. Model Cities was conceived, in part, as a self-help program to enable the poor to have the power of decision over their own immediate environment. Reaffirming this theme, Martin cautioned that the Model Cities Program would improve the lives of the elderly only if they are active in local planning and program operations. The committee, accordingly, recommended stepped-up funding for projects to organize the elderly and involve them in Model Cities programs.[1] This study concludes one such project.

That many of the "maximum feasible participation" projects have failed is now well known. Our findings will indicate reasons for these failures that have not, we believe, been fully recognized in the experience of other reported projects. Since the special focus of this project is the urban elderly poor, we begin on that theme.

Acknowledgments

We thank those on the aging project staff and our consultants who have worked with us through the thirty-nine months encompassed in the study of the urban elderly poor. The list includes Richard D. McKelvey and Richard G. Niemi of the University of Rochester; Michael R. Coveyou of Iowa State University; Gloria M. Gioia, community organizer, and her field aide, Ruth Stark of the Citizens Planning Council; Alonzo Jones, community process analyst, Citizens Planning Council; Catherine Diringer, Marti Bucci, and Jackie Fields, research aides, Citizens Planning Council; Wanda Walker, secretary, Citizens Planning Council; Ford Tucker of Strong Memorial Hospital; Boris H. Mikolji of Rochester Institute of Technology; Gordon F. Streib of Cornell University; and Kenneth J. Smith of the University of Miami. In earlier phases of the work we benefitted from the help of Roger M. Weir of State University College at Brockport, and Janet T. Hinckley and Charles F. Biggs of the Citizens Planning Council.

For financial support we thank the Administration on Aging of the Department of Health, Education and Welfare. In particular we want to thank Marvin J. Taves, Ryland Swain, David Dowd, Jessie Gertman, and their support personnel.

Facilities and other assistance were provided by Irving Norry, St. Matthew's Church, and William J. Allen. Rolland R. Michael provided invaluable help throughout the project. We thank anonymously the subjects of our study—the urban elderly poor—and our team of interviewers and part-time helpers. And we accord special thanks to Marcelle Levy, special advisor to the governor of the state of New York on the problems of the aging.

Last, but not least, we thank our cheerful and efficient typists, Peg Gross and Janice Brown. Although all of the above named persons contributed their advice or help at various phases of the study, the responsibility for the final statement, of course, must rest with the authors.

1

An Overview of Aging

What began as a study of the elderly poor in Rochester's Model Cities area at once became a study of race relations as well. Both the multiracial character of the inner city and the replies obtained in a survey of the elderly revealed that the issue of race was unquestionably the most salient concern in the daily lives of the aged, especially for the white residents. To overlook the racial dimensions of aging would preclude a comprehensive understanding of the preferences of the elderly poor, their social action potential, and the likelihood that programs designed in their behalf can succeed. And, most important of all, it would omit a consideration of the fact that the conditions of the black and white aged are radically distinct. It means one thing to be a poor, old, white, inner-city resident and yet another to be black.

This study thus synthesizes two lines of inquiry: (1) What is the behavior of the elderly poor in the inner city? and (2) How does the multiracial, inner-city environment affect the aged? This chapter undertakes a brief review of knowledge about the aged and the ways they have been studied. The next chapter examines the characteristics of the inner city that was designated as the Model Cities neighborhood area in Rochester; here we identify and describe the target population. The remaining chapters disclose our findings and what we believe are cogent recommendations for programs affecting the aged poor.

The Place of the Elderly

Much has been written about the role of the elderly in American society, and of their growing future importance. There are over twenty million individuals who have passed their sixty-fifth birthday, and millions more in the preretirement age of fifty-five to sixty-five.[1] The number of Americans sixty-five years and over is more than six times as great today as it was in 1900. Moreover, it is estimated that

1

by the year 2000 there will be more than twenty-eight million people who are over sixty-five

Life expectancy at age sixty-five is presently about fifteen years. This figure is expected to rise significantly in the near future as breakthroughs are made in controlling diseases that afflict the aged. The numbers of the very old over seventy-five years should increase at about twice the rate of the over-sixty-five group as a whole, and at more than twice the rate of the total population. The political power of the elderly, if it is mobilized, has the potential for significant growth. At present the aged constitute 15 percent of the eligible voters, but that figure will rise to about 25 percent in the next few decades.

One crucial fact for many of the elderly is that old age is synonymous with poverty. In 1966 half of the families headed by persons sixty-five and over had incomes of less than $3,700, which is less than half the median income attained by younger families. The median income for the group of five million aged who live alone was $1,443 in 1967. Of the seven million elderly families, about two out of five had incomes of less than $3,000 a year, while half of these latter had less than $2,000 a year. About five million older Americans fall below the poverty level. Moreover, elderly people form a growing proportion of those living in the central city. The aged poor have been unable to join the flight to the suburbs of younger, more affluent citizens and thus concentrate in inner cities because of the presence of inexpensive housing. As the quality of life in downtown areas continues to deteriorate, the central city will become more and more the locus for the aged poor.

The twentieth century has especially seen a dramatic increase in the numbers of aged blacks in the United States.[2] Between 1900 and 1967, the expectation of life at birth increased by 28.6 years for black males and 35.0 years for black females to 61.1 and 68.2 years respectively. Their white counterparts showed gains of only 19.6 and 24.0 years. Thus the problems of aging will increasingly affect members of the black community.

If there is any group of the aged that require special assistance, they are found in the inner city where financial circumstances force blacks and whites into impoverished integrated neighborhoods. This study thus directly analyzes the economically worst-off segment of the elderly. What we learn from these people will determine if any measures can be taken to improve their social welfare.

Gerontology: The Study of Aging

The field of gerontology reflects a multidisciplinary interest. The social and behavioral scientists who study aging come from such diverse fields as sociology, psychology, political science, economics, business administration, and social work. It is generally acknowledged, though, that sociologists have predominated in studies about the aged.

Until recently, many sociologists appeared to be almost exclusively concerned with confirming, modifying, or disproving the "disengagement theory" that was explicitly set forth by Cumming and Henry in 1961.[3] In capsule form, Cumming and Henry assert that since death is universal and inevitable, both society and the individual must adjust themselves to this fact to avoid disruption and disequilibirium and maintain homeostasis in the social system; this is accomplished through gradual and mutual disengagement which is completed at death. The thesis of disengagement posits that an individual's death, if unprepared for, is dysfunctional for the social system, and hence a functional way of preparing for death is to disengage.

The disengagement thesis captured the attention of a good many researchers in studies of gerontology. Some tried to distinguish between voluntary and involuntary withdrawal and their comparative impact on morale and attitudes;[4] some focused on the value changes that accompany aging in an effort to show that the elderly are disillusioned with increasing age and therefore seek an accommodation with reality;[5] still others question whether age itself or the impact of physical and social stress that increases with age produce disengagement.[6] In an exhaustive review of the entire literature surrounding the disengagement debate, one scholar concludes that many investigators reject the disengagement theory as a universal, inevitable process, even though they include it as one of a number of successful routes toward old age—often the disengagement theory is consistent with observation, at other times not.[7] Two authors, who exemplify this continued concern with the disengagement thesis, offer the concept of *differential disengagement,* by which they mean that disengagement occurs at different dates and in different amounts for different people at different times.[8] They conclude from a seven year study of retirees "that disengagement theory must be further refined to emphasize that in real life, differential disengagement is the common pattern . . . . disengagement in one sphere, such as retirement, does not signal withdrawal and retrenchment in all spheres.[9]

A competing approach in studying the aged is referred to as the "activity" theory.[10] This theory asserts a positive relationship between activity and life satisfaction. Interpersonal activity would thus be important for predicting an individual's sense of well-being in later years. Although a number of scholars have reported that activity is important for predicting life satisfaction among the aged, an attempt to construct an axiomatic statement of activity theory led three scholars to conclude that none of the hypotheses relating frequency of activity to life satisfaction received consistent empirical support.[11]

. . . the more general conclusion from this study is that the data provide surprisingly little support for the implicit activity theory of aging which has served as the theoretical base for practice as well as research in gerontology for decades.[12]

These scholars caution that neither activity nor disengagement theory by themselves can adequately account for optimal aging. The shortcomings of these theories does not lie in their logical constructs, but in the variability of aged individuals and their different value systems, personalities, physical, and social situations. Overgeneralized theory building becomes, of necessity, a dangerous task.[13]

Political scientists have also explored the problems of the aged, focusing, mainly, on two aspects of political behavior: (1) old-age movements that are established for specifically political objectives, e.g., the Townsend Movement,[14] the California Institute of Social Welfare;[15] and (2),the social and psychological characteristics of aged voters.[16] The first set of studies examines the aged as a political interest group. Noting that the aged poor are marginal to the main stream of American political life, most analysts conclude that effective political activity on their behalf requires the support of groups which have a more secure base in the community. Put another way, active elderly people should join with people of all ages to solve problems of joint concern, instead of just forming a group of their own.

Notions of disengagement or withdrawal implicitly underlie

research on the political behavior of the aged. Among the major beliefs are these: political interest declines after the sixties (but that people in their seventies and eighties are more active than young people in their early twenties); partisanship among the aged is more determined—only half as many people are independents at age sixty-five as at age twenty; the aged are less supportive of change or appeals for change; the aged are the most committed group in the population to traditional party attachments, almost equally divided between the Republican and Democratic parties; and from society's point of view, many people do not want the aged to get involved in political activity. It is generally believed that the elderly poor do not command the political clout to act as effective advocates on their own behalf.

Our thinking and preparation owes much to the published works of sociologists and political scientists, but it is clear that an eclectic approach now governs gerontological research. It is now a hallmark of many articles and books to call for the development of a theory that systematizes the extant empirical work. Additionally, there has been an overemphasis on middle-class, chiefly white, retirees when compared with rural, black and other ethnic minorities, or the inner-city poor in general. The 1971 White House Conference on Aging report on "The Aging and Aged Blacks" emphasized the fact of significant black underrepresentation at the conference. The authors of the report were concerned over the lack of attention given to minority groups *even* for the formation of issues presented in the background materials and the workbooks for discussion and policy recommendations at the conference.[17] We contend that those aged least in need of assistance have been most thoroughly studied; those in greatest need least studied. Two priority areas in the field of gerontology are easily recognizable: (1) a concern for theoretical rigor, and (2) an emphasis upon the urban elderly poor (of all races).

Research Procedures

To derive from a set of axioms an internally consistent body of theorems which systematizes our knowledge about the processes of aging or the political efficacy of the aged is not an easy task. Moreover, the multiracial inner-city poor, a relatively neglected subpopulation, form a more formidable challenge than suburban retirees or institutionalized whites. We focused exclusively on that more difficult community, the inner-city aged, an element of the population perhaps most in need of study and material aid. We have relied chiefly on the technique of survey research to study these aged poor. Before describing our technical procedures and some of the difficulties we encountered, however, we want to make explicit the theoretical notions that governed the development of our interview schedule.

It has recently become fashionable to berate the failures of the welfare programs undertaken in quest of the "Great Society." Some analysts of various federal antipoverty programs have concluded that city political machines often gained control over these well-intentioned programs and subordinated them to the existing power structure; accordingly, the poor in the ghettos were barely helped at all. The general thesis of these critics is that government agencies may be unable to carry through successfully a serious program of community social action when such a program involves confronting the forces that most resist change. The goals of many of these programs were clearly stated: to provide more services to the poor, to create more opportunities for them, to help the poor to help themselves via their own participation, and to give them leadership opportunities. Although these programs were not successful, in some ways they revealed middle-class America's wish to transform the poor into socially constructive, happy middle-class citizens with white suburban values.

Indeed, the very concept of "helping" the poor, the elderly, or the black, i.e., providing more services and opportunities for them, implies that their present consumption falls short of some socially optimal level. That level is of course, white, middle-class suburbia. Gerontological research has often sought to determine the *needs* of the elderly. Specific recommendations for assistance have generally rested upon middle-class norms, couched in language that appeals to middle-class administrators or social workers. One rarely encounters the view that the aged poor have a life style which its participants actually prefer to that of middle-class retirees. Instead, it would be fair to say that research about the *needs* of the elderly is predicated upon a set of values which asserts that it is socially desirable to convert the aged poor into aged middle-class citizens.

The point of this discussion is to explain how we chose to conceptualize and present our understanding of the aged poor.

"Problems of old age are of two general kinds: those that older people actually have and those that experts think they have."[18] We wanted to avoid the bias displayed by those latter experts who first assess in some objective terms the *needs* of the elderly and then recommend public spending programs to meet those *needs*. To avoid that bias entails keeping our personal, middle-class values separate from our understanding of the aged poor. To maintain this distinction, we borrowed from economic theory the notion of "rational man."

The notion of rational man can be construed as a summary statement of human nature that reads as follows: people act in their own self-interest. Although self-interest is often equated with wealth-maximizing behavior, or pecuniary motives, it is not exclusively synonymous with the single minded pursuit of money. Some people maximize nonpecuniary goals; e.g., philanthropy, the giving away of money. To say that people act in their own self-interest is simply to say that individuals are able to rank their preferences from most- to least-preferred and can select that option highest on their list. This is what the economist means when he says that people are maximizers of utility—they select the available option that provides for them the greatest satisfaction. To analyze human behavior, economists ask what the self-interest of the relevant participants to any action involves.

For us, the critical aspect of this conception of rational man is that each individual defines his own self-interest *subjectively*. This implies, of course, that individuals have and can express preferences. Moreover, subjectivity implies that there are no such things as *correct* preferences. This point is crucial and cannot be overemphasized. What may be a correct preference for one person may be anathema to another. Preferences are personal valuations based on whatever principles, values, and tastes an individual may hold, however acquired. It has yet to be demonstrated, except to those accepting knowledge by revelation, that an objectively correct preference exists for a person except from his own point of view. To say that an individual is able correctly to order his preferences is not to say that he has the "truth" for others. Hence, the only correct concept of preference is from the subjective standpoint of the individual.

This conception of man as a utility-maximizing individual leads directly to the following question: how do the aged maximize utility? or, in the laymen's words, what gives the aged satisfaction?

What do they want? It is logically incorrect to ask: what do they need? The concept of *need* denies the subjective nature of individual preference. From the standpoint of middle-class America the aged poor may *need* a considerable increase in the provision of certain goods and services. However, the elderly poor, from their standpoint, may not consider these items desirable, especially the elderly members of racial or ethnic minorities. Therefore, we do not hold up any arbitrary standards against which we can measure the physical or psychological *needs* of the elderly.

To cite only one example, by way of anticipation, it is true that most of the elderly we studied were *poor* by middle-class standards. However, only a small percentage expressed a desire for subsidized services. Most, instead, yearned for old-fashioned neighborhoods in which it was safe to walk the streets at night. Many of the elderly whites even expressed a desire for the pre-World War II segregated neighborhoods when few minority group members lived among them.

While we do not set forth an explicit theory of the processes of aging, or of the political, psychological, or physiological correlates of aging, we have been very careful to formulate our thoughts and design our research instruments around the notion of subjectivity. From this point of view, the aged are identical with persons of all ages who make choices and seek satisfaction from them. Only an earlier birthdate distinguishes older from younger persons. The preferences of the aged are thus as valid as those of any other persons as revealed in response to a properly worded questionnaire, or as determined by making inferences about preference orderings on the basis of observation.

The subjectively determined "preference" notion thus governed the design of our research. Rather than try to identify the *needs* of the elderly, we sought, instead, their preferences on items deemed important on the basis of previous research. We carefully selected questions that would allow us to evaluate the disengagement-activity controversy, explore political involvements, and uncover if interest for voluntary community action were present among the aged, among others. (A copy of the questionnaire appears in Appendix A.)

The Survey

As mentioned at the outset, this study is an analysis of the elderly poor living in the Model Cities area. To ascertain the preferences of this population, we conducted a sample survey of aged persons over fifty-five in Model Cities. In the fall of 1971 we enumerated the target area for the purpose of drawing a systematic sample. Aged persons in every fourth household were identified and a comparison with 1970 census data on age, sex, and race parameters confirmed the accuracy of our enumeration. On the basis of this enumeration, a computer designated random sample of 402 target cases was selected for interviewing. This sample size balanced consideration of cost with statistical reliability. Of that number, 332 were completed, virtually all between August 1971 and February 1972.[a] In some cases our interviewers made as many as eight to ten callbacks. We employed special multilingual interviewers familiar with the cultural backgrounds of respondents of German, Polish, and Ukranian descent. Quality control was performed on over 10 percent of the interviews which included one or more follow-ups on interviews completed by each of the sixteen different interviewers we employed. We might note that most of the interviewers we hired and trained were indigenous to Model Cities.

An earlier version of the interview schedule was pre-tested in July 1971. Many of the interview items that were borrowed elsewhere in order to replicate the work of other scholars proved incomprehensible to our respondents. Thus we changed many questions from a closed answer agree-disagree form to open-ended in character.

Although the following chapters will evaluate the disengagement-activity debate, and explore the political ramifications of advancing age, our major findings and their policy recommendations concern the multiracial environment of the inner city. This result was not by the choice of the investigators, but stemmed from the discovery that race proved to be a dominant component in virtually every response given by the elderly. As the elderly poor become an increasing proportion of central city residents, an understanding of their situation becomes more important. Growing racial polarization and hostility between blacks and whites will make the plight of the elderly poor of both races as unwilling captives of their impoverished neighborhoods even more precarious.

---

[a] The potential sample was reduced to 366 cases by deaths and emigrations from Model Cities. We thus successfully interviewed over 90 percent of the designated sample.

2

The Aged Poor and Their Environment

There is ample reason to believe that the city will be the site of racial struggle in the years to come. Mechanization of southern agriculture, the general lack of other employment opportunities, and substantially more attractive welfare arrangements have encouraged large numbers of blacks to move off the land and into the northern cities of the Midwest and East. A black majority already populates the nation's capital and projections for 1985 show that black majorities will inhabit many of our large cities: Chicago, Philadelphia, St. Louis, Detroit, Baltimore, New Orleans, Cleveland, even Richmond and Jacksonville.

Though the percentages are not yet so dramatic, the same process is occurring in Rochester. In 1950 there were 7,590 blacks in a city of 332,488. Blacks increased to 23,586 ten years later while the city declined overall to 318,611. Blacks more than doubled to 49,647 by 1970 in the face of a dramatic citywide reduction to just under 270,000. These trends are continuing today and have also been accompanied by a steady growth in the Puerto Rican population. If these trends continue, Rochester may join many of the nation's urban centers that have non-white population majorities.

It should be pointed out that suburban Monroe county, excluding Rochester, has virtually no black residents. Approximately 500 lived in suburban Monroe County in 1960 and this figure grew to only about 2,500 by 1970; the white suburban population grew by well over 100,000 during the same period. As blacks have moved into the inner city in large numbers, whites have rushed to the suburbs in even greater numbers. Whole sections of the city have become increasingly black while the suburbs remain lily-white. This description will, in all likelihood, remain intact for at least the next decade or more.

Blacks now comprise more than 18 percent of the population in Rochester. They are not, as indicated, evenly distributed throughout the city. Instead, they are disproportionately concentrated in the older, more dilapidated sections of town with white neighbors who either cannot afford to escape to the suburbs or find their twenty- to forty-year-old attachments to the neighborhood too difficult to break.

The Model Cities Neighborhood area typifies the black areas in Rochester. It also typifies Model Cities areas across the nation. The area consists of a portion of the inner-city bounded north by Clifford Avenue, on the east by North Goodman Street, on the south by Main Street and the Inner Loop and on the west by the Genesee River. It is, like other Model Cities areas, a transitional and declining locale.[1]

The Model Cities Program in the United States[2]

The 1966 Demonstration Cities and Metropolitan Development Act was passed by the United States Congress in the wake of the turbulent summers that began in 1963 in the streets of Rochester and then spread to Watts (Los Angeles), Detroit, Cleveland, Gary, Nashville, Newark, and other American cities. This legislation established Model Cities Programs in a number of cities throughout the United States.

Typically, the program called for the creation of a Model Cities Field Office in each participating city, with a director and planning staff. These were to be responsible to designated city officials, e.g., the mayor, and their activities were federally financed. Generally, an area in the inner city containing a disproportionate number of poor and ethnic minority persons was chosen for the project. The program envisioned that interested citizens and existing neighborhood organizations would interact to establish planning groups within the area.

The idea behind Model Cities was to allow the neighborhood to make a concerted and coordinated attack on such problems as housing, health, municipal services, recreation, transportation, education, welfare, social services, crime, law enforcement, economic development, and employment problems. Neighborhood planning groups with the aid of the Model Cities Field Office were to draw up proposals for programs in selected areas of concern for approval by the city and the federal government. Following approval, the Model Cities Field Office was to coordinate the local and federal bureaucratic agencies that must implement the programs. In short, the Model Cities Program was conceived as an attempt, via comprehensive and coordinated planning, to restore balance to a selected community of the less well-to-do, giving, it was intended, considerable decision-making power to the beneficiaries themselves.

Model Cities in Rochester

Model Cities in Rochester exemplifies the purposes of the national program. More than 50 percent of the inhabitants are black, about 15 percent Puerto Rican, and less than 40 percent white. According to census figures, the total population in Model Cities has declined from 45,055 in 1950, to less than 40,000 ten years later, and is just barely more than 35,000 on the date of the 1970 census. The corresponding black figures are 3,848, 9,878, and 17,746. Blacks now comprise an absolute majority and the remaining members of the white community increasingly see themselves as a beleaguered group. Though whites make up the majority of Rochesterians, and especially an overwhelming majority in Monroe County, Model Cities' whites are a racial minority and see themselves in that light.

Figures 2-1 through 2-3 vividly reveal the changing racial character of a portion of Rochester's inner city. From an initial black concentration in census tract 91, black in-migration has produced substantial non-white majorities in many of the adjacent tracts. The changing racial composition from the 1970 census date through 1973 has further accentuated the increasing predominance of the black and Puerto Rican communities. An analysis of many of the nation's other Model Cities areas would undoubtedly yield similar results. The increasingly precarious position of the decreasing white inhabitants, a disproportionate number of whom are aged retirees, renders our study all the more compelling. These aged are daily witnesses to the major social happenings of urban America: crime, congestion, dilapidated housing, a declining economy; they are, as well, present-oriented with neither the time nor hope for a better future. In addition, the black immigrants to these areas are dispossessed, poor, and often an angry group, who came to the city to better themselves but met barriers on the way up to this betterment.

Model Cities and the Elderly[3]

One of the intents behind the launching of the Model Cities program

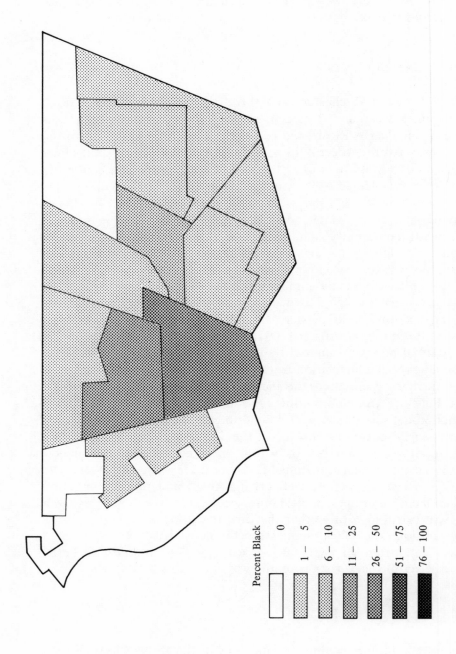

Figure 2-1 Model Cities Census Tracts, Rochester, New York, 1950

Percent Black

0

1 – 5

6 – 10

11 – 25

26 – 50

51 – 75

76 – 100

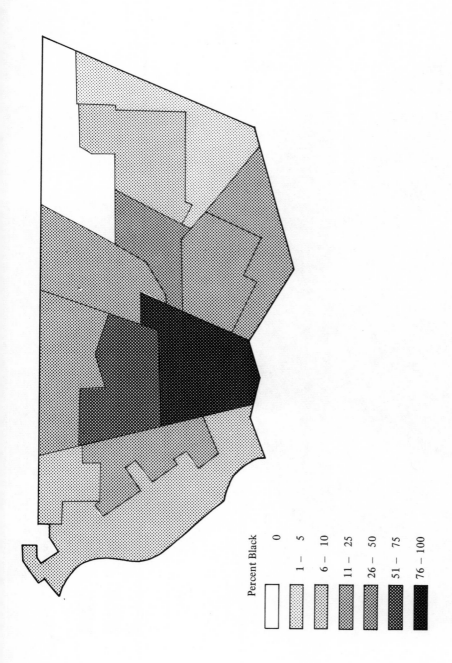

Figure 2-2 Model Cities Census Tracts, Rochester, New York, 1960

Percent Black

0

1 – 5

6 – 10

11 – 25

26 – 50

51 – 75

76 – 100

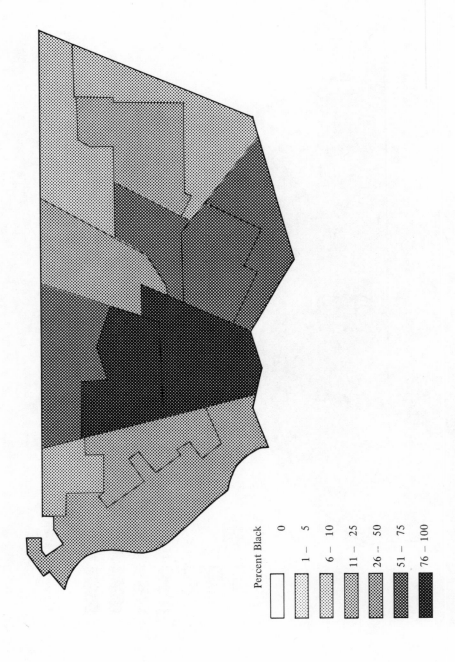

Figure 2-3 Model Cities Census Tracts, Rochester, New York, 1970

Percent Black

0

1 – 5

6 – 10

11 – 25

26 – 50

51 – 75

76 – 100

in 1966 was the belief that it could contribute significantly to improving the lives of the elderly. The program's comprehensive approach to such problems of the aged as housing, health, and transportation offered hope that the high percentage of elderly inner-city inhabitants would become major beneficiaries.

In July 1970, the Department of Housing and Urban Development and the Administration on Aging (of the Department of Health, Education and Welfare) entered into a joint contract with the National Council on the Aging to provide technical assistance in programming for older persons in twenty-one designated Model Cities. Four purposes underlay this joint endeavor: (1) organization of the elderly to facilitate their involvement in Model Cities programs, (2) evaluation of existing programs, (3) assistance in implementing programs which have already been funded, and (4) assistance in coordinating resources.

Rochester was selected as a site for a research and demonstration project that would attempt to organize the elderly to facilitate their involvement in Model Cities planning. This was not a capricious selection. As a result of the Older Americans Act of 1965, the executive department of the New York State Office for the Aging had already approved and funded the establishment of a Department of Aging within the structure of the Council of Social Agencies. Its purposes were threefold: identify the elderly, ascertain their concerns, and coordinate community services working on their behalf. In 1970, with encouragement from the state, the Administration on Aging funded a project to evaluate the problems of older people in such areas as housing, protective services, and transportation in Model Cities. It was also designed to test the idea of the possibility and extent of self-help by the elderly poor, thereby laying the groundwork for the federally financed project that constitutes the basis of this book.[4] Funding under the subsequent grant enabled us to ascertain specifically who were the aged poor in Model Cities, to assess their subjectively perceived individual concerns, and to determine their willingness and capacity to participate in and plan for community services. We turn, then, to a description of these aged poor; here we will learn what it means to be a black or white old person in Rochester's inner city.

The Aged Poor

According to an earlier survey, Puerto Ricans make up about 15 percent of Model Cities' inhabitants, but almost 90 percent of them are under fifty-five years of age.[5] Reflecting this age pattern is the fact that our sample included only ten elderly Puerto Ricans, a number too small to permit comprehensive analysis. Appropriately, then, we generally confine our discussion throughout this book to the aged black and white inhabitants of Model Cities.[a]

Our study covered not only "the aged," that is those sixty-five and over, but those approaching old age, men and women in the fifty-five to sixty-five age bracket. We chose to include the younger group as well because we wanted to learn about the processes of aging; this would help to anticipate the behavior of the future aged in the Model Cities area. The following analysis of the elderly whites in Model Cities is taken from 247 completed interviews; of blacks, 75. Females are a majority in each race: 68 percent of the interviewed blacks are female compared with 58 percent for whites, though this difference is not significant. Age patterns are also racially variant—compare the significant fact that 27 percent of the aged white are seventy-five years and over with a corresponding figure of 4 percent for blacks. Black residents, on the average, are younger than whites. These age patterns for males and females of both races are displayed in Table 2-1. The notable absence of blacks above age seventy-five is probably attributable to the fact of their lower life expectancy and more recent settlement in the neighborhood, the latter shown momentarily. For white males, the pattern is reversed; males are the majority only among those over seventy-five.

The basic theme which underlies this study is, as we have stated,

Table 2-1
Model Cities Inhabitants, by Age, Race, and Sex (by percentages)

Age	(N=102) White Males	(N=145) White Females	(N=24) Black Males	(N=51) Black Females
55-59	16.7	15.9	25.0	39.2
60-64	12.7	19.3	33.3	13.7
65-69	24.5	19.3	25.0	23.5
70-74	11.8	23.4	12.5	19.6
75+	34.3	22.1	4.2	3.9

[a]In the discussions that follow, all cited percentages referring to significant differences have been tested for statistical significance.

that the race factor is critical for understanding the behavior and attitudes of the elderly poor. In order to study the effects of advancing age upon political, social, or psychological dimensions of aging, it is necessary to see when and where blacks and whites are similar, and when and where they are distinct. The first comparison is present employment status.

Table 2-2
Employment Status by Age (by percentages)

	(N=67) 55-59	(N=60) 60-64	(N=75) 65-69	(N=60) 70-74	(N=70) 75+
Employed full time	47.8	28.3	4.0	3.3	1.4
Employed part time	1.5	1.7	2.7	1.7	1.4
Housewife	7.5	10.0	8.0	18.3	12.9
Not employed	43.3	60.0	85.3	76.7	84.3

Disengagement, as a notion of occupational withdrawal, aptly suits Table 2-2. Just under half of the fifty-five to fifty-nine age group are employed fulltime. In the next age bracket, sixty to sixty-four, only half as many are employed, and among those sixty-five and over, only about 3 percent are employed. We were surprised to discover no significant difference in the incidence of unemployment between blacks and whites, as shown in Table 2-3. This table also shows that black women do not view themselves as housewives, a response that reflects the different economic experiences of the black female; few black women have enjoyed the luxury of housewife status in their lifetimes.

Moreover, the occupation of the chief wage earner in the respondents' households reflects the menial or unskilled employment that the vast majority of blacks have experienced—over 70 percent fill or have filled service and unskilled positions. Contrast this with a

Table 2-3
Employment Status by Race (by percentages)

	(N=247) Whites	(N=75) Blacks
Employed full time	16.6	17.3
Employed part time	0.8	5.3
Housewife	13.4	2.7
Not employed	69.2	74.7

figure of only 26 percent for whites among whom skilled and professional persons are three to four times more prominant than blacks. None of the aged black are (were) managers, proprietors, or clerical personnel, and only a handful are (were) professionals, foremen, or skilled artisans.

It is not hard to account for low job status among blacks. Among other factors, their educational background was not conducive to skilled employment or professional careers. Table 2-4 reveals, for instance, that over half of the black respondents had completed six or fewer years of school. Less than 6 percent graduated from secondary school. Small wonder, then, that blacks are consigned to menial and unskilled jobs. Although whites, on average, are some-what better educated, only a handful have attended a college or university with just one-tenth holding high school diplomas. These differences correspond, though, to the better jobs held and now occupied by whites. Political and market discrimination, as well, have worked against the interests of blacks.

Table 2-4
Educational Attainment by Race (by percentages)

	(N=247) Whites	(N=75) Blacks
Primary school or less	45.3	52.0
Less than high school	36.0	41.3
Less than high school/ some technical school	6.1	1.3
High School	8.1	2.7
High School/some technical school	0.8	—
Some college	0.4	—
College or University	1.2	—

Younger interviewees, afforded greater income from full-time employment, report household incomes higher than for older respondents. About 30 percent of those aged fifty-five to fifty-nine claim family incomes in excess of $8,000, a figure that tapers off steadily to around 11 percent for those over seventy-five years. Racial differences, as asserted, are very pronounced. Table 2-5 shows that almost half of black households report a total family income of $2,000 or less, compared with 13 percent among whites. Above $5,000, the figures are reversed: 39 percent white, starkly con-

Table 2-5
Total Family Income by Race (by percentages)

	(N=247) Whites	*(N=75)* Blacks
Less than $2,000	13.7	48.0
Less than $3,000	34.8	70.7
Over $5,000	38.9	14.7

trasting with under 15 percent black. A designation of the poverty level at $3,000 annual income places 71 percent of black households in poverty, but only 35 percent of white households. Blacks are evidently financially worse off than whites.

Table 2-5 also reflects differences in sources of income by race. Our survey reveals that nearly 40 percent of whites' income is derived from wages, the balance attributable to social security and pension payments. Only two whites in the entire 247 report receiving welfare. This reflects an "old-fashioned" independence ethic. Despite refusing welfare, these elderly whites have incomes superior to those of the blacks. For blacks, 33 percent derives from wages, 44 percent from social security and pension stipends, but nearly 23 percent depends on welfare. Blacks are distinctly worse off, less mobile, more dependent, poorly educated, and have a lower than average life expectancy.

With particular regard to the black family, much has been made of its supposed instability. Our analysis shows many broken marriages (see Table 2-6). Divorce and separation among blacks are

Table 2-6
Marital Status by Race (by percentages)

	(N=247) Whites	*(N=75)* Blacks
Single	5.3	6.7
Married	57.1	37.3
Separated/divorced	4.9	25.3
Widowed	32.8	30.7

five times greater than for whites. Since the incidence of single or widowed status is about the same, the chief difference between black and white households is the relatively greater proportion of unbroken white marriages. That the percentages of widowed among whites is not substantially higher than blacks confirms the greater life expectancy among elderly whites, given the significantly greater proportion of whites over age seventy.[6]

Household size complements the divorce and marriage profiles of each race. About one-quarter of each race live in households containing three or more persons. However, 65 percent of whites live in two person households compared with 40 percent for blacks; correspondingly, higher separation and divorce rates are reflected in the fact that 35 percent of the black respondents live alone versus 23 percent of whites. As well, the income differences over varying household size show a marked racial effect. Over 53 percent of all large (three or more persons) white households report annual incomes of more than $8,000; the corresponding black figure is 5 percent. And, it is notable that large black households have incomes comparable to smaller ones (see Table 2-7).

The changing character of Model Cities is easy to pinpoint. Table 2-8 affirms that the majority of white residents have lived in their present accommodation for more than fifteen years; over a fifth for

Table 2-7
Income by Household Size by Race (by percentages)

| | Whites | | |
Income	One Person (N=56)	Two Persons (N=133)	Three + Persons (N=58)
Under $1,000	1.8	1.5	1.7
$1,000 to $1,999	32.1	6.8	5.2
$2,000 to $2,999	39.3	20.3	5.2
$3,000 to $3,999	14.3	26.3	3.4
$4,000 to $4,999	1.8	10.5	8.6
$5,000 to $5,999	5.4	6.0	12.1
$6,000 to $6,999	1.8	8.3	1.7
$7,000 to $7,999	–	1.2	2.0
Over $8,000	3.6	18.0	53.4

| | Blacks | | |
Income	One Person (N=26)	Two Persons (N=30)	Three + Persons (N=19)
Under $1,000	26.9	20.0	10.5
$1,000 to $1,999	38.5	20.0	26.3
$2,000 to $2,999	19.2	26.7	21.1
$3,000 to $3,999	7.7	16.7	10.5
$4,000 to $4,999	–	3.3	5.3
$5,000 to $5,999	–	6.7	5.3
$6,000 to $6,999	–	6.7	10.5
$7,000 to $7,999	3.8	–	5.3
Over $8,000	3.8	–	5.3

more than forty years. Blacks display an opposite pattern—nearly half have lived in their present home less than five years. The census figures that appear earlier in this chapter show the growing and recent migration of blacks into Model Cities, with a corresponding white exodus. But those whites who remain have occupied their homes for the goodly part of their adult lives.

Table 2-8
Tenure of Residence by Race (by percentages)

	(N=247) Whites	(N=75) Blacks
0 to 5 years	15.8	44.0
6 to 15 years	21.9	37.3
16 to 40 years	40.1	14.7
over 41 years	22.3	4.0

Home ownership, as might be expected, is basically a white phenomenon. About 78 percent of the whites own their own homes, with a median value in the $10,000 to $12,500 range. Nearly 55 percent of white-owned homes range in value from $7,500 to $15,000; for blacks the corresponding figure is under 19 percent. Nearly 79 percent of black citizens in Model Cities are renters and cannot afford to buy what are for them expensive homes. Not a single black owns a home valued over $15,000. And, we should note here that these higher-valued, white-owned homes are not overly concentrated in just a few sections of Model Cities. Expensive homes are also found in the racially mixed areas and in the predominantly non-white portions. The racial composition of Model Cities has changed more quickly than the value of houses in the all black sections would lead one to expect. Owners of higher valued property are frequently found in mixed or chiefly black sections as in virtual white neighborhoods.

It remains to mention that 95 percent of the blacks are Protestant, whereas 75 percent of whites are Catholic. Religious differences, thus, reinforce racial divisions. Although the effects of advancing age are universally evident in reduced employment, somewhat lower income and, with one exception, greater longevity of women, the effect of racial difference is dramatic. Whites are wealthier, better educated, own their own homes, have better jobs, retain more stable households, are more established in the neighborhood, and are independent of welfare. Blacks, on the other hand, are worse off, live

Table 2-9
Value of House by Race (by percentages)

	(N=247) Whites	(N=75) Blacks
Don't own home/rent	21.9	78.7
$0 to $4,999	–	1.3
$5,000 to $7,499	1.6	1.3
$7,500 to $9,999	17.8	5.3
$10,000 to $12,499	17.4	12.0
$12,500 to $14,999	19.8	1.3
$15,000 to $17,499	8.5	–
$17,500 to $19,999	9.3	–
$20,000 to $24,999	3.2	–
Over $25,000	0.4	–

in less satisfactory accommodations, are poorly educated, engage in menial employment, have more broken marriages, have a larger proportion on public assistance, and represent the more recent arrivals in the area. We thus have *two worlds of aging: black and white*. In the following chapters we examine their differing social preferences, racial values, physical concerns, and explore the implications of these facts for alternative forms of assistance directed at the elderly poor, or possibly organized by the poor themselves.

3 A Profile of Elderly Concerns

Among America's elderly population, the inner-city poor unquestionably encounter the greatest financial and personal hardships. Scholarly research discloses and social workers reveal intensive involvement with a small number of carefully defined problems that generally plague the elderly poor: transportation, meals, medical care, visiting with friends and family, quality of housing, adequate employment opportunities, provision for voluntary tasks, and psychological disposition, e.g., the "correlates of satisfaction."[1] Those not owning cars have difficulty getting around and the minimal standard of material consumption stands out in stark contrast to that of the affluent white suburbanite. Our description of the inner-city black and white aged at the end of the previous chapter suggests that here is to be found that subgroup of the elderly most in *need* of basic services.

But recall the discussion of need in Chapter 1; there we emphasized the importance of adopting a subjectively defined view, voiced by the elderly themselves, of what they want, of what they consider personally important. We want to avoid the imputation of middle-class norms that invariably accompanies the term *needs* and therefore we were painstakingly careful to insure that our questions (see Appendix A) elicited only the subjective preferences of the elderly. This care produced a startling result: the vast majority of the elderly do not consider themselves to be in *need* of substantial services or personal assistance. In fact, the percentages indicating concern with basic services almost seem unreasonably low, given our a priori expectations and the results of other research. Only 16 percent of the respondents report difficulties with transportation; 14.5 percent find getting meals problematic; 19.6 percent have trouble seeing a doctor; 6.3 percent do not see their friends often enough; 12.3 percent are unhappy with the house or apartment in which they live; only 3.3 percent are presently looking for work (most are voluntarily retired and only 1 percent of those not looking for work believe that the lack of jobs prevents their securing employment); and only 4.2 percent do volunteer work (mostly with church-related organizations), and the remainder are not looking for volunteer work. The low percentages persist despite the fact that 73.8 percent of those interviewed report such specific health problems as hearing and sight defects, ulcers, high blood pressure, arthritis, diabetes, bad legs, health ailments, and cancer.

It is indeed striking that only a small proportion of the inner-city elderly poor express a need ("want" in our terms) for basic services. Although by our standards the elderly poor face hardships getting around and making ends meet on limited incomes, they generally *do not* perceive themselves to be living in deprivation. It should come as no surprise, then, that public services which blanket a fixed geographical area have only minimal impact on those most wanting. Indeed, services delivered in blanket form are often wasted from the perspective of their supposed intent. Given that charitable resources are scarce, it is imperative that programs designed to benefit the elderly poor must first locate those with genuine material wants. Too often these resources are consumed in ways not intended by those planning for the needy.[2]

Recall that blacks, on average, possess considerably fewer resources than whites. If money permits the purchase of those goods and services that provide personal satisfaction to the elderly, then a disproportionate number of those reporting problems should be black. Table 3-1 vividly confirms the two disparate worlds of aging. The rate at which blacks report problems is from two to eight times as frequent as whites. Among the urban elderly poor, blacks are most wanting. Further analysis shows that the higher incidence of black problems is not the result of living alone—percentage rates hold constant across single person, two person, and large households.

The value of public or private programs for the urban elderly poor

Table 3-1
Concerns of the Aged Poor by Race (by percentages)

	(N=247) Whites	(N=75) Blacks
Problems with Transportation	12.6	25.3
Trouble getting Meals	5.7	42.7
Trouble seeing Doctor	15.8	28.0
Problems visiting Family	21.1	32.0
Unhappy with Homes	9.3	22.7

is now called into question. Need as defined by middle class values has a degree of effect. Blacks, by social service standards, are more in need as revealed in their higher expressed level of wants. However, as Table 3-1 shows, most blacks do not express wants on issues most closely related to financial deprivation. Almost three-fourths do not consider transportation a problem. Nor is housing seen as a problem by about 77 percent of the blacks, despite the fact that half of all black households have under $2,000 each year of disposable income, and 70 percent live well under the poverty level of $3,000.

A first-hand look at those sections in Model Cities in which these poverty-level blacks live raises doubts about the analysis of the survey (or our own sensibilities). Yet we are convinced that their replies are valid. The correct inference to be drawn from these data is that inner-city blacks, and poor whites for that matter, see and accept life on entirely different terms than middle-class intellectuals who write books about them. Our data emphatically point to this difference, alarming though it may be.

Race clearly conditions the existence and degree of perceived wants. Is the same true for advancing age? To check for any effects we examined for each age group the degree of expressed concern over transportation, meals, visiting with friends and family, medical care, and general health. The results appear in Table 3-2. Transportation problems accompany advancing age and health evidently deteriorates somewhat, but, surprisingly, advancing age diminishes food and medical care problems. On the crucial dimension of medical care, those over seventy-five report half as much difficulty securing adequate medical treatment as those in the fifty-five to fifty-nine

Table 3-2
Concerns of the Aged Poor by Age Group (by percentages)

	(N=67) 55-59	(N=60) 60-64	(N=75) 65-69	(N=60) 70-74	(N=70) 75+
Problems with Transportation	10.4	13.3	18.7	13.3	22.9
Trouble getting Meals	16.4	15.0	14.7	15.0	11.4
Poor Health	7.5	11.7	16.0	31.7	25.7
Trouble seeing Doctor	26.9	21.7	17.3	18.3	14.3
Problems visiting Family	32.8	18.3	17.3	16.7	30.0

bracket. Among the Model Cities elderly there is, in general, no consistent relation between advancing age and increasing wants.

A control for race shows that within each advancing age bracket, blacks report more problems than whites. Race, not advancing age, is the key predictor of who seeks or can benefit from programs of assistance set up on behalf of the urban elderly poor. Altogether, though, the aged poor of both races do not feel deprived. An earlier study in Model Cities discovered that the percentages of persons reporting no problems increased with age (see Table 3-3).[3] Thus, we cannot expect an overwhelming majority of aged persons to vociferously demand more services or improved facilities.

Although this chapter is brief, its two conclusions are all the more profound. First, the expressed level of *need* is minimal, and the self-reliant values of the aged whites hint that it would require special ingenuity to design programs these elderly would accept and participate in. Second, those expressing the most needs are clearly the old blacks. The elderly whites are unlikely to work with these older blacks on any advocacy program as the next chapter attests.

We turn now to the psychological dimension of aging that is often referred to as "life satisfaction," "happiness," or emotional well-being. The psychological well-being of the aged poor is severly constrained by the deteriorating urban and hostile racial atmosphere in which they live. We will show that the racial problem overwhelms the conventionally specified set of transportation, medical and food problems and, perhaps, prevents the implementation of successful programs. Let us look, then, at our two worlds of aging: black and white.

Table 3-3
Respondents with "No Problems" in Rochester's Model Cities (1969) by Age (by percentages)

Age	No Problems	
15-24	25.5	(N=63)
25-34	22.6	(N=120)
35-44	30.2	(N=116)
45-54	29.5	(N=74)
55-64	40.4	(N=57)
65+	43.4	(N=60)

Source: Richard S. Sterne, *Social and Health Services in the Model Cities Area, Rochester, New York* (Rochester, N. Y.: Council of Social Agencies, 1969), pp. 11-17. (mimeo)

4

Perspectives on Race: Two Worlds of Aging[a]

Model Cities in Rochester is, in many ways, akin to the classical notion of the "plural society," "comprising two or more elements or social orders which live side by side, yet without mingling, in one political unit."[1] Although Furnivall was describing Indonesians, Chinese, Burmese, and Europeans in pre-World War II Burma and the Netherlands Indies, his definition aptly fits Rochester's Model Cities area in the early 1970s, and probably most of the multiracial Model Cities areas across the nation. Differences in income, level and type of education, religion, upbringing, and marital patterns all reinforce the culturally distinct values that separate urban elderly blacks from whites. And perhaps the differing racial attitudes held by blacks and whites most sharply differentiates the two elderly cultures. Although the subjects of this chapter are old people, our emphasis came, through the nature of our data, to the character of race relations in the inner city rather than the processes of aging per se. The racial issue conditions interpersonal relations, affects the values and beliefs of the elderly including their expressed wants, and bears upon the likelihood that they will participate in any integrated program set up in their behalf. The racial element underpins, almost determines, the emotional make-up of elderly whites, complicating the integration of the inner city. We saw in Chapters 2 and 3 how the living standards of blacks and whites vary; now we show how their values and attitudes contrast even more sharply.

General Views on Aging

It is customary for scholars and social workers to ascertain the elder person's views on retirement. Does, for example, the retiree view himself as a member of a select population that should undertake joint action on matters of common concern to the elderly? Such

[a]This chapter was prepared with the assistance of Richard D. McKelvey.

questions as "should the old retire to make room for the young?" "can old people solve common problems by working together?" and "do old people share common problems?" typify the intent to see the elderly as an integrated community.[2] If the presupposition that the elderly share common problems and that collective action leads to greater success than disaggregated individual efforts is correct, then distinctions of race demand serious study.

We asked the opinions of our respondents to the above questions. Their replies show strong racial variants. Blacks are more willing to retire from their jobs (85 percent) to make room for the young than whites (69 percent). This may be attributable to the observation that the menial and unskilled jobs they hold are less attractive (and more willingly given up) than the higher status and prestige positions which whites surrender on retirement.

What are the self-expressed prospects for social action initiated by the elderly? The replies of whites and blacks again diverge sharply. The impact of race on general views of aging appears in Table 4-1.

Table 4-1
Attitudes Toward Aging by Race (by percentages)

Question	(N=247) Whites	(N=75) Blacks
Do old people share common problems?	50.8	76.0
Can old people solve common problems by working together?	61.1	88.0

Three-fourths of the black respondents profess that old people share common problems and fully 88 percent of them believe that these problems can be solved by working together. The corresponding percentages for whites are 51 and 61 respectively. Independent of the need for interracial cooperation, old blacks display a greater inclination toward collective action than old whites, a conclusion reached in an earlier study.[3] This inference is consistent with the social behavior of the aged: 27 percent of the elderly black belong to social clubs, a figure that falls below 20 percent for whites. Curiously, the rate of white male participation is double that of white women; so also is that of black female participation (see Table 4-2). This latter pattern may reflect the black female's greater

Table 4-2
Social Club Membership by Race and Sex (by percentages)

White Males (N=102)	27.5
Black Males (N=24)	20.8
White Females (N=145)	14.5
Black Females (N=51)	29.4

occupational experience compared with that of the white elderly housewife who retains her home-centered orientation.

We have seen that interest in collective action varies by race. What about the prospects for multiracial collective action? The answer to this question is vital for those who advocate that the aged should organize themselves to more effectively express their wants, or for those who wish to aid the elderly with advocacy measures. We addressed this issue directly.

What about a community action group of older citizens? If one were formed in your neighborhood, would you be interested in joining it? (A Community action group is a group that gets together to solve common problems.)

Two-thirds of the black respondents expressed positive interest, but only 18 percent of the whites replied in the affirmative.

Racial Attitudes

To probe the possibility that whites and blacks would join a common group, we examined the willingness of blacks and whites to associate with each other on a series of specific relationships. With regard to employment, 23 percent of the whites said they would not like to work on the same job with blacks; only 4 percent of the blacks expressed the corresponding dislike of whites. As to social activities, 35 percent of the white respondents did not like the notion of common membership in clubs or organizations with blacks, whereas fewer than 3 percent of the blacks expressed disdain about integrated social clubs. Evidently, black separatism does not pervade the elderly black community. When asked specifically about membership in clubs for older people to which members of the other race also belonged, 35 percent of the whites compared with only 5 percent of the blacks replied no. That blacks are more willing to join with whites in collective social activity seems compatible with the more broadly expressed black conviction that old people can solve common problems by working together. On the other hand, whites are less enthusiastic about the prospects for joint action and resist intensely the notion of cooperation with blacks. Racial antipathies appear to be almost entirely one-sided.

The friendship patterns that predominate among the interviewees (see Table 4-3) further confirm these findings. All but 4 percent of the white respondents restrict their friendships racially, unlike blacks, who are much more out-going. Two-thirds of the blacks claim white persons among their friends. Neighborhood informants interpreted these figures for us. Friendship to a black is loosely defined, e.g., a white person who allows a black to enter a bus first is seen as a friend in the eyes of a black. Whites more narrowly define friendship to intimate relationships. Thus, the black world of interpersonal relations is both more comprehensive and more tolerant; the white view more restrictive and hostile.

Table 4-3
Racial Composition of Friends by Race (by percentages)

	(N=247) *Whites*	*(N=75)* *Blacks*
All White	80.6	—
Mostly White	15.4	—
All Black	—	33.3
Mixed	4.0	65.3

Stereotypes

To better understand the underlying beliefs that condition interracial contact, we tried to obtain a picture of the stereotypes each race holds of the other. Using a technique that one of us employed in another multiracial society, we asked our respondents to judge both white and black people on such personal dimensions as intelligence, thrift, responsibility, cleanliness, honesty, and ambition.[4] Special attention was paid to the precise wording of the questions to prevent any possible misunderstandings. We coded the replies to such questions as "do you think most Whites try to get ahead? How about Blacks?" or "do you think most Whites are smart? How about Blacks?" high, low, or neither. A simple yes or no response seemed safer and analytically more valid than a less conservative effort to establish degree of highness or lowness. Since this question came at the very end of the interview, we felt that sufficient rapport had developed to encourage frank replies. Indeed, the interviewers were barraged with volunteered information beyond the simple "high" or "low" response. Many of the elderly eagerly shared their views with us on this question.

The image that each race holds of itself and the other comprises Table 4-4. Several patterns vividly show up. First, whites rate themselves much more favorably on every attribute than blacks. Second, with one exception, blacks see themselves less favorably than they picture whites. The unattractive view of the black held by whites is reinforced by the black self-portrait. Blacks generally give whites a more favorable image than whites ascribe to themselves. The only exception to this trend and it is marginal at best, involves the dimension of honesty. Whites rate themselves low, and blacks rate themselves above whites. However, even here blacks are more generous to whites than are whites to blacks.

To state the matter somewhat differently, old blacks reflect an image of the white as smart, responsible, and ambitious, beyond what whites attribute to themselves. Whites, on the other hand, subscribe to an image of the black that is even less flattering than the black self-portrait. The import of these racial stereotypes is now clear in light of the previous discussion: blacks are willing to join with whites in collective activity but the white view of the black, on the contrary, does not predispose him toward interracial cooperation. Antipathy, not harmony, is the general feeling. It is quite possible, of course, that by restricting these racial portraits to the over fifty-five population we might have obtained slightly different replies. But these beliefs have not been so recently formed that older persons might be expected to assign radically different stereotypes to older and younger blacks. In sum, the resistance of whites to the notion of integrated clubs, work or joint social action shows up in the racial

Table 4-4
Racial Stereotypes by Race (by percentages)

INTELLIGENCE

	High	Low	Neither
Whites rating Whites	55.5	7.3	37.2
Whites rating Blacks	12.6	40.5	47.0
Blacks rating Whites	58.7	21.3	20.0
Blacks rating Blacks	53.3	25.3	20.0

THRIFT

	High	Low	Neither
Whites rating Whites	45.7	20.2	34.0
Whites rating Blacks	10.1	51.4	38.5
Blacks rating Whites	77.3	8.0	14.7
Blacks rating Blacks	52.0	30.7	17.3

RESPONSIBILITY

	High	Low	Neither
Whites rating Whites	29.6	21.1	49.4
Whites rating Blacks	6.1	50.6	43.3
Blacks rating Whites	49.3	17.3	33.3
Blacks rating Blacks	44.0	24.0	32.0

CLEANLINESS

	High	Low	Neither
Whites rating Whites	56.3	5.7	38.1
Whites rating Blacks	8.5	45.7	45.7
Blacks rating Whites	49.3	32.0	18.7
Blacks rating Blacks	41.3	37.3	21.3

HONESTY

	High	Low	Neither
Whites rating Whites	27.9	20.6	51.4
Whites rating Blacks	6.5	47.8	45.7
Blacks rating Whites	33.3	45.3	21.3
Blacks rating Blacks	36.0	41.3	22.7

AMBITION

	High	Low	Neither
Whites rating Whites	74.5	2.8	22.7
Whites rating Blacks	33.2	36.0	30.8
Blacks rating Whites	88.0	4.0	8.0
Blacks rating Blacks	60.0	28.0	12.0

Note: The table is read as follows. For example, 55.5 percent of the whites rate whites as high in intelligence, 7.3 percent of whites rate themselves low in intelligence, and so forth.

values they profess. Conversely, black interest in multiracial pursuits conforms with the favorable picture of whites they project.

Residential Proximity

To this point, we have seen that the racial stereotypes projected by the elderly complement interracial friendship patterns. But interracial contact more directly affects some of the Model Cities inhabitants than others. Recall that Model Cities contains a large proportion of blacks (and Puerto Ricans) who are more densely settled in some census tracts in the heart of Model Cities than on the fringes of the area. We determined from the interviews the racial character of the immediate neighborhood in which each respondent lives and, after corroborating those estimates with the observations obtained through special field research, we developed Table 4-5.

Table 4-5
Racial Composition of Neighborhood by Race (by percentages)

	(N=247) Whites	(N=75) Blacks
All White	12.6	—
Mostly White	30.4	4.0
Mixed (about half and half)	44.9	22.7
Mostly non-White	4.9	24.0
All non-White	7.7	49.3

Almost half of the aged whites live in multiracial mixed neighborhoods, with one-eighth on predominantly non-white blocks. Blacks, either by choice, economic necessity, or discriminatory reasons, live chiefly among their own kind; only 4 percent of them reside chiefly in what are still basically white neighborhoods.

What effect does interracial living have on the emotional disposition, fundamental values, and the willingness of the elderly to entertain multiracial social activity? We began by asking each respondent if he was happy with his immediate neighborhood. Almost equal percentages of blacks (29) and whites (33) expressed displeasure with their neighborhoods. But, as the racial composition of the neighborhood becomes increasingly black, white displeasure dramatically rises. The percentages displayed in Table 4-6 are extremely provocative. Whites living on blocks with few or no blacks are happy with their neighborhood. Those unhappy more than

Table 4-6
Racial Composition of Neighborhood by Happiness with Neighborhood for Whites (by percentages)

	Unhappy	Happy
All White (N=31)	16.1	83.9
Mostly White (N=75)	14.7	85.3
Mixed (N=111)	38.7	61.3
Mostly non-White (N=11)	72.7	27.3
All non-White (N=19)	73.7	26.3

double as the neighborhood takes on an evenly mixed racial tone. Finally, three out of four whites are unhappy living in what are virtually black (or Puerto Rican) neighborhoods, a rate of unhappiness about fivefold greater than for whites living in white-majority areas.

A similar analysis for blacks does not disclose a strong relationship between residential propinquity to whites and happiness with the neighborhood. In a follow-up question we asked where each respondent would most prefer to live. Of those whites wishing to remain in the same house, 90 percent are happy with their neighborhood; 80 percent of those who would rather move from their present home are unhappy. For blacks, unhappiness with the neighborhood was expressed not in terms of escape from the area, but in the desire to see improvement in the physical character of the area and greater personal security.

We saw earlier that the racial attitudes held by members of the white community do not encourage or support voluntary interracial cooperation or integration. The generally unfavorable white-held stereotypes of blacks is further exacerbated for those whose unhappiness with their neighborhood derives from their being, or at least feeling, compelled to live among blacks. We compared the stereotypes of those happy and unhappy whites to ascertain if the presence of blacks in large numbers improved or worsened those images. Unhappiness with neighborhood for whites increased by 16 percent the perception of blacks lacking in ambition, increased dishonesty (as might be expected) 30 percent, and reduced the already unfavorable images for cleanliness, responsibility, thrift, and intelligence from 20 to 26 percent. In other words, integrated living experience dramatically raises the hostility toward and the displeasure with one's black neighbors. Whites living in chiefly white areas hold a more favorable view about the black. In this case, interracial interaction does not promote social harmony; instead, familiarity breeds contempt.

Table 4-7
White Racial Stereotypes of Blacks by Happiness with Neighborhood (by percentages)

	(N=81) Unhappy	(N=166) Happy
Blacks Low in Ambition	46.9	30.7
Blacks Low in Honesty	67.9	38.0
Blacks Low in Cleanliness	63.0	37.3
Blacks Low in Responsibility	67.9	42.2
Blacks Low in Thrift	66.7	44.0
Blacks Low in Intelligence	54.3	33.7

A similar result emerged from white responses to the following question:

Some say that blacks have been trying to get ahead too fast. Others feel that they haven't gotten ahead enough. How about you? Do you feel that blacks are trying to get ahead too fast, are they going too slowly, or are they moving about the right speed?

None of the white respondents felt that blacks were moving ahead too slowly. But 57 percent of those who are happy with their neighborhood feel that blacks are getting ahead too fast compared with the much higher figure of 79 percent for those not so content.

Was it possible that the strong impact of race might be partly spurious, given that race is strongly related to certain economic and social variables which might themselves be significant? For example, that whites in predominantly black neighborhoods are less satisfied than whites in mixed or predominantly white neighborhoods might simply reflect the fact that the housing in black neighborhoods is more dilapidated and run down, property values have fallen drastically, and crime and vandalism is more serious. Perhaps these factors, and not the racial composition of the neighborhood, produce individual dissatisfaction with one's neighborhood. To the extent that economic variables and race are correlated, it is difficult to distinguish the independent effect of each of these variables. Sufficient differences in these variables exist, though, for us to evaluate these interrelationships.

However, one cannot really address this analysis with contingency tables due to the diminishing cell size when more than two or three controls are introduced. It was necessary, then, to perform a multiple regression analysis on the data (see Table 4-8). The regression

Table 4-8

Multiple Regressions of Happiness with Neighborhood on Neighborhood Composition and Various Economic and Social Problems†

	Model 1		Model 2		Model 3	
	Whites	*Blacks*	*Whites*	*Blacks*	*Whites*	*Blacks*
NBHCOMP	−.32*	−.01	−.26*	.01	−.19*	.04
MEDVAL	.10	.19	.08	.05	.07	.08
MEALTR			.04	−.02	.03	−.02
TRANSPO			−.02	−.08	−.05	−.06
DOCTPR			.08	.06	.07	.15
NBHPR			−.38*	−.55*		
RACEPR					−.47*	−
CRIME 1					−.36*	−.44*
CRIME 2					−.19*	−.43
HOUSEPR					−.14*	.06*
OTHERPR					−.15*	.50*
R^2	.14	.03	.28	.34	.34	.43

† Entries are standardized beta coefficients.

* Indicates significance at the .05 level.

analysis yields estimates of the independent impact of each of the independent variables on the dependent variable. Along with neighborhood composition (NBHCOMP) and median value of the housing (MEDVAL), the independent variables include measures of individual perceptions of problems associated with deteriorating economic and social conditions. First are the strictly physical difficulties associated with getting meals (MEALTR), transportation (TRANSPO), and medical attention (DOCTPR). Second is a variable measuring perceived problems with the neighborhood (NBHPROB) which, in turn, has been disaggregated in the last two regressions into the two categories of general crime against property and specific crimes affecting personal safety (CRIME 1 and CRIME 2), racial problems (RACEPR), housing problems (HOUSEPR), and other miscellaneous problems (OTHERPR).

The figures reported in Table 4-8 are the standardized regression coefficients that emerge from the regression analyses. The standardized regression coefficients represent the change (in standard deviations of the dependent variable) to be expected when a change of one standard deviation is made in the independent variable. The usefulness of using standardized coefficients is that it allows direct comparison of the relative importance of different variables in the equation. Thus, the larger the standardized regression coefficient, the larger the effect of a unit change (in standard deviations) of that variable in explaining the dependent variable. Those variables with the largest standardized coefficients, then, account for the bulk of the explanatory power. Also reported is the R^2, or the coefficient of determination, which is a measure of the explanatory power of the model. The R^2 represents the proportion of the total variance of the dependent variable accounted for by the regression. We have indicated with an asterisk (*) those coefficients that are statistically significant at the .05 level.

Table 4-8 shows, among whites, that neighborhood composition remains important after controlling for other economic and social problems. Economic conditions and strictly physical problems are of minor importance compared with neighborhood composition and other neighborhood problems. The original effect of racial composition in model (1) is somewhat attenuated in model (2), due to the inclusion of other neighborhood problems, but still has an independent impact. Racial considerations are even more evident for whites when perceived neighborhood problems are identified (model 3). Much of the explanatory impact of neighborhood problems is attributable to the perceived racially based problems. Whites are disturbed about the black influx into their neighborhoods, and these qualms are not at all completely explained by the accompanying economic and social deterioration of the neighborhood. Sharp differences arise between blacks and whites in these regressions. Model (1), consisting of neighborhood composition and a control for economic value of the housing, explains 14 percent of the variance among whites, but next to nothing among blacks. Neighborhood composition thus has no significant effect in either direction among blacks. What then do blacks want? Models (2) and (3) indicate that blacks want better living conditions—they are bothered by crime and other neighborhood conditions, but do not care about the neighbor-hood's racial composition.

Other interesting differences between blacks and whites emerge in the stereotype images that are held of blacks. Table 4-9 reports a

Table 4-9
Stereotype Rating of Blacks†

	Ambition	Intelli-gence	Honesty	Clean-liness	Responsi-bility	Thrift
	Whites Rating Blacks (N=246)					
HN	−.14*	−.16*	−.26*	−.24*	−.27*	−.24*
CATHOLIC	−.11	−.02	.08	.05	.05	−.03
STATUS	.02	.14*	.08	−.02	.07	.02
INC	−.05	.06	.01	−.04	.00	.02
RC	−.05	−.07	.01	.06	.05	−.07
R^2	.03	.05	.08	.05	.07	.05
	Blacks Rating Blacks (N=74)					
HN	−.02	.10	−.02	−.06	−.04	.01
CATHOLIC	−.01	.01	−.25*	.11	.14	−.04
STATUS	.23	−.27*	−.38*	−.32*	−.26*	−.12
INC	.12	.05	.17	.19	.10	.06
RC	−.13	−.09	−.21	.11	−.01	−.16
R^2	.09	.07	.27	.19	.11	.04

† Entries are standardized beta coefficients

* Significant at .05 level

regression of various socioeconomic status type variables on stereo-type scores. We included happiness with neighborhood (HN), racial composition of neighborhood (RC), total family income (INC), a dummy variable for religion (CATHOLIC), and a status variable (STATUS) that measured whether the individual was economically above or below the mean in his neighborhood. Although none of the regressions explain a large portion of the variance, the most consistently important variable for whites is happiness with neighbor-hood; for blacks, status. Those whites who are happiest with their neighborhood see blacks most favorably. For blacks, a rise in economic status is associated with a less favorable perception of their own kind.

Implications

These results became curious in light of our discovery that whites adhere to a more positive view of human nature than blacks. About 71 percent of the whites, compared with 60 percent for blacks, feel that people in general care about helping others. Yet, for this specific collection of black neighbors, whites put forth a generally poor image, which deteriorates even more as immediate proximity to blacks increases. The more that blacks and whites are forced into integrated neighborhoods, the more these images should continue to disintegrate.

Can we make a chronological inference from this cross-sectional analysis? Earlier we pointed to the changing racial composition of Model Cities during the past twenty years, and we have also noted that most whites are relatively long established in private homes compared with the more recently arrived blacks who rent. Accordingly, the white experience of living in chiefly black neighborhoods is relatively new. The inference to be drawn is clear: as elderly whites become a still smaller minority in Model Cities, their stereotypes of blacks will undoubtedly grow less attractive. The single most important concern of the older white person is the one over which he has the least control—the racial factor. Service wants (needs), by comparison, pale in importance. Whites want, more than any other social service, a service no agency in Rochester will provide—to remove the blacks who have become their neighbors.

The prospects for multiracial collective action are thus very dim and diminish with each passing year. The solution to the racial problem for the elderly in Model Cities will probably come in later years when old whites will have moved out or died off. But that only means the problem will shift to other, not yet racially homogenous, sections of the city in which older residents concentrate.

A desirable and practicable solution is unclear and the political role of the elderly in it uncertain. But we can make some reasoned guesses about the types and degrees of political activity the elderly are likely to consider, given their available resources. That consideration is the topic of the next chapter.

5 The Politics of the Elderly Poor

Advocates for the elderly point to the potential political clout that twenty million organized Americans could command. Yet the power implied in these numbers has not materialized. Earlier research demonstrates that the Democratic and Republican parties have taken the elderly for granted. Research also shows that the aged are less supportive of change or appeals for change; they are the most committed group in the population to traditional party attachments, being almost equally divided between the Republican and Democratic parties; partisanship is more solidified—only half as many people are independents at age sixty-five as at age twenty. Previous studies suggest, moreover, that political interest declines continuously after the sixties. All these considerations dilute the potential power of the elderly. Among all sections of the population, the elderly are perhaps least well-organized and the least able to articulate their preferences over the public allocation of goods and services.[1]

More to the point, most analysts assert that the aged *poor* are especially marginal to the main stream of American political life. It is generally claimed that the elderly poor are unable to produce any political clout to act as effective advocates on their own behalf. Solutions to the problems of the elderly poor require, in this view, that the elderly merge their efforts with people of other ages to solve common problems. To form limited groups of aged persons for the resolution of age-specific problems is believed less efficacious than garnering support from groups which, having a more secure basis in the community, focus on broader problems.

Organizing the elderly poor alone is thus seen as an exercise in futility—*unless* we can demonstrate their potential for political action. Portions of the survey we conducted were designed to ascertain the extent of ability for and actual participation in social action among the multiracial, elderly poor. In this chapter we focus on the foundations of any action by the elderly poor: their political knowledge or awareness, their interest in politics, their interest in collective political action, their attitudes towards politics, their political behavior, and, finally, an appraisal of their actual potential efficacy in the area of political action.

Political Attitudes: Cognitive and Affective Elements

The study of attitude theory and measurement generally focuses upon three underlying dimensions that comprise the internal structure of attitudes.[2] The first two, the affective and cognitive elements, are discussed in this section; the third, the behavioral element, comprises the next.

The study of attitudes can be a field unto itself, but more often scholars attempt to link specific attitudes with predicted forms of behavior. Important attitudes were uncovered in the previous chapter. We therefore now ask what effect prejudice has upon the likelihood of multiracial cooperative behavior? We want specifically to test the notion of political activity by the elderly poor.

A first set of questions tapped the cognitive component of political attitudes: what level of political information and awareness have the elderly attained? Predictably, almost every respondent recognized Richard Nixon—only 4 percent did not. The vice--president, Spiro Agnew, was unknown to 29 percent of the sample, and 37 percent could not identify George Wallace, despite his recent political prominence. Beyond these national personalities, the elderly within Model Cities were less cognizant of a host of inner-city programs and agencies. FIGHT in Rochester, for example, is a well-publicized black social action group, which also has a factory operation. It was, however, known only to about 27 percent of the sample. More startling, indeed, is that only 15 percent could correctly identify something called "Model Cities"; a full 55 percent have never heard of Model Cities and the remaining 30 percent have only a vague notion of its presence in their neighborhood. Action for a Better Community (ABC), another prominent local organization, was correctly identified by only 6 percent of the respondents. These three institutions—political, economic, and social—remain invisible to the majority of elderly poor. To involve the aged in Model Cities' planning decisions borders on the questionable when but one of seven old people even knows of its existence. How many could possibly know the intent, purpose, and procedures, much less the

accomplishments, of Rochester's Model Cities program?[3] Of course
one function of the Model Cities administration is to make itself
known, to educate its resident population, and to stimulate their
interest in participating in decisions. The Rochester Model Cities
program was about four years old when the survey was taken, which
suggests that it still has a long way to go to attain its publicity goals.

To this point we have described the limited information and
awareness of community programs of the elderly poor. Consistent
with the theme of this book, blacks and whites evince different levels
of awareness. For instance, almost twice as many blacks as whites
recognize George Wallace: 56 percent to 33 percent respectively.
Knowledge of specific inner-city programs that specifically serve
blacks is much richer among black respondents, by a factor of two to
one (see Table 5-1). A majority of whites could neither identify

Table 5-1
Political Information Among the Elderly Poor by Race (by percentages)

Knowledge of		(N=247) Whites	(N=75) Blacks
F.I.G.H.T.	No	51.4	25.3
	Somewhat	26.3	30.7
	Yes	22.3	44.0
ABC	No	64.8	65.3
	Somewhat	30.8	24.0
	Yes	4.5	10.7
Model Cities	No	51.4	64.0
	Somewhat	32.4	25.3
	Yes	16.2	10.7

FIGHT nor ABC. A somewhat larger proportion of whites than
blacks recognized "Model Cities," though the majority are not well
informed nor perhaps care. Blacks, then, are more cognizant of
specifically black-oriented programs and agencies. (Recall that blacks
want more social services and willingly express interest in collective
social action.) White elderly poor acknowledge national personalities,
but possess little information about and show little interest in
community activities.

Evidently the dissemination of information to neighborhood
residents has lagged behind the intentions of the planners. Perhaps
we mistakenly assume that persons with little education easily digest
public information. Table 5-2 shows that higher education leads to

Table 5-2
Political Information by Education (by percentages)

Knowledge Of		(N=191) 0-7 yrs	(N=67) 8 yrs	(N=39) 9-11 yrs	(N=26) 12 yrs	(N=9) 13+ yrs
Wallace	No	48.7	28.4	17.9	15.4	—
	Somewhat	23.0	31.3	28.2	26.9	11.1
	Yes	28.3	40.3	53.8	57.7	88.9
F.I.G.H.T.	No	59.7	31.3	25.6	30.8	—
	Somewhat	21.5	32.8	30.8	34.6	55.6
	Yes	18.8	35.8	43.6	34.6	44.4
Model Cities	No	66.5	43.3	35.9	38.5	22.2
	Somewhat	25.7	37.3	33.3	38.5	33.3
	Yes	7.9	19.4	30.8	23.1	44.9

political information. Note that correct recognition of George Wallace more than triples, awareness of FIGHT more than doubles, and that knowledge of Model Cities quintuples when those with postsecondary education are compared with those having no more than a primary school experience. Further note the totals in each education category. Almost 60 percent, that is 191 persons, have no more than seven years of formal education. Political interest depends, perhaps, upon political information and the majority of elderly poor are poorly educated and therefore poorly informed.

This discussion of political information or awareness, the cognitive element of attitude structure, now gives way to a consideration of the affective/evaluative dimension. In order to tap this dimension, we borrowed several questions from scales that were constructed to measure such concepts as "alienation," "civic competence," "citizen duty," etc. Attempts to apply the complete scales did not succeed. We found that the questions, even when tested by highly skilled interviewers, were incomprehensible to the elderly residents in Model Cities. However, we employed a small number of select questions which accurately reveal the political commitments of the elderly poor.

How important is the vote? About 48 percent of the sample believe that if a person doesn't care how an election comes out, he shouldn't vote in it. Put another way, if the issues in or outcome of the election are not salient to the elderly poor, almost one of two do not believe that the responsibility of "doing your citizen duty" compels participation. A slightly larger proportion, 51 percent, believes that public officials don't care about what "people my age think." Further, 48 percent profess that "people my age" don't have any say about what the government does. Government and its agents, the public officials, are givens in the community life of the elderly poor. They are not amenable to senior citizen pressure in the view of these seniors. Indeed, when it was suggested that "Sometimes politics and government seem so complicated that a person my age can't really understand what's going on," fully 84 percent agreed.

A portrait of political indifference, at times bewilderment, suggests that we delve deeper. Accordingly, we asked "Why do you think some people your age are not involved in politics?" The largest group, 43 percent, think that the elderly lack political abilities. The next largest category, 22 percent, admit to a lack of interest; 13 percent have no faith in the political process while 10 percent give no reply. Only 13 percent insist that old people are actually involved in politics.

When asked "What would make public officials listen to older citizens?" only 23 percent recommend that the elderly organize neighborhood groups. Recall from Chapter 4 that only 18 percent of the white respondents express positive interest in joining a community action group of older citizens; conversely, two-thirds of the blacks express interest. These figures confirm how concretely political attitudes vary by race. Although equal proportions of whites and blacks (about 85 percent) believe that politics is too complicated for the ordinary old person to understand, race sharply differentiates adherence to the concept of citizen duty. Over 60 percent of the elderly whites believe that one should vote, even if he doesn't care about the election. Among blacks only a significantly smaller 28 percent subscribe to the citizen duty norm. In the absence of important electoral issues, blacks do not hold much store in the act of voting itself. As to racial evaluations of social agencies, 46 percent of whites believe them good, a figure that drops to 31 percent for blacks. This negative view of social agencies by the majority of each race is not likely to incline them toward seeking more services.

That education enhances political information suggests a similar effect on the affective/evaluative dimension of attitudes. Sixty-seven percent with seven or fewer years of formal schooling believe that voting is still important even when one's preferred outcome is unlikely, a figure that rises steadily to 89 percent among the best educated. Similarly, 91 percent of the least educated subscribe to the "complex politics" view of the world; among the best educated, only

56 percent believe politics too complicated to understand. The two factors of race and education thus bear upon the evaluative dimension of political attitudes. Blacks are more indifferent to, yet willing to participate in, politics. Whites, by contrast, assert the citizen duty ideal, but show less interest in concrete collective action. Further analysis (not displayed) confirms that the responses among all categories of respondents are internally consistent. When elections are deemed important, or the individual's vote is held to be important as a matter of principle, the overwhelming majority subscribe to the citizen duty ethic even when one's preferred candidate is likely to lose. As expected, those who accept the "vote in principle" doctrine disproportionately think that public officials care about the views of the elderly (70 percent). By stark contrast, 65 percent of those interviewees who think electoral abstention appropriate in the face of disinterest believe that public officials do not care. The aged poor, in the language of the social psychologist, do not suffer cognitive dissonance. The attitude clusters that comprise the individual's mental set are consistently linked among the elderly poor.

Political Behavior

But it is easy to say one thing and do another. To uncover any such discrepancies, we asked our respondents not only how they felt about politics, but also what they did about it. Is the reported behavior of the older poor person consistent with his voiced, or stated, political outlook? Do those with higher interest, stronger affect, and more extensive political knowledge participate more intensively? Do they vote at a higher rate? Do they contribute to campaigns, talk about politics, assist candidates, or do they simply claim the citizen duty norm yet abandon it in practice? Table 5-3 provides a first answer to these questions.

Note a strong relationship between reported turnout and belief in citizen duty. In the 1968 presidential election, and the 1970 gubernatorial and senatorial elections, about two-thirds of the elderly *voters* firmly emphasized the importance of voting as an act in and of itself. The corresponding majority of nonvoters do not believe that voting is important when election interest is absent. Here we find that behavior is consistent with underlying belief: the old do what they say they should do.

Table 5-3

The Relationship of Voter Turnout to Concern About Elections (by percentages)

		(N=249) Voters	(N=83) Non-Voters
1968 Presidential Election	Should Vote	63.0	19.3
	Should not Vote	37.0	80.7
		(N=209)	(N=123)
1970 Gubernatorial Election	Should Vote	64.6	30.9
	Should not Vote	35.4	69.1
		(N=200)	(N=132)
1970 Senatorial Election	Should Vote	66.0	27.3
	Should not Vote	34.0	72.7

Does voting in a presidential or state election convey anything more than a once-in-every-two-or-four-year expression of citizen duty? In 1968, for example, 72 percent of the sample reported pulling a lever in the voting booth; 69 percent claimed a similar effort in the 1970 elections. But the standard political participation index contains such additional factors as talking to people about politics, attending political meetings, or working on behalf of a candidate. What about the elderly poor? Do they do more than vote? Apparently not. Less than 10 percent report talking about politics with other persons, fewer than 5 percent ever attend political meetings, and only 3½ percent admit working for a political candidate. The conventional wisdom that the aged are not an organized group commanding the political clout of sheer numbers seems well-confirmed among these inner-city poor.

Throughout this study the racial factor significantly confirms our views of two worlds of aging. Table 5-4 shows how dramatically racial differences affect the extent of political participation. Black abstention in the 1968 presidential election is significantly higher than white, but white and black abstention are comparable in the 1970 state elections. These figures are not surprising. What is surprising is that participation beyond the mere act of voting is more a black than white phenomenon, especially given results which ascribe to blacks greater political indifference. Three to four times as many blacks as whites, proportionately, do more than just vote, yet

Table 5-4
Political Participation by Race (by percentages)

	(N=247) Whites	(N=75) Blacks
Voted in 1968 Presidential Election	75.1	61.4
Voted in 1970 Congressional Elections	68.4	69.3
Discussed Politics	6.5	20.0
Donated Money	5.7	28.0

these same blacks, on average, are more alienated with a lower sense of citizen duty and citizen efficacy. Although we do not have a ready explanation for this result, the implications are somewhat more evident. The greater rate of black elderly participation, conjoined with the greater black expressed willingness to organize for collective action, promises better prospects for coherent group organization among elderly blacks, assuming the organizational problems can be solved. The acute minority position of the elderly whites in the Model Cities area may explain their relatively low level of political involvement among this population, even while they articulate the traditional ideal of citizen duty. Old whites in Model Cities are not likely to dominate the local elections that specifically bear upon their districts; they commensurately express little interest or involvement.

As mentioned at the outset, the old are most resistant to change; coherent group action is not very likely to strike a responsive chord in either the Democratic or Republican parties. Robert Binstock puts this point clearly.

While most politicians wish to avoid offending the aged, and many favor proposals to provide incremental benefits to older persons, few are disposed to develop special appeals to the aged among the central issues of their campaigns. They regard the partisan attachments of the aged to be among the most stable within the American electorate, not likely to be shifted substantially by special appeals.[4]

Political party identification is shown in Table 5-5. Note that substantially similar percentages of whites claim Republican and Democratic sympathies. Blacks, on the other hand, by a three to one ratio, express a Democratic preference. Even more important were

Table 5-5
Political Party Identification by Race (by percentages)

	(N=247) Whites	(N=75) Blacks
Not Registered	13.8	8.0
Republican Party	35.6	21.3
Democratic Party	41.7	61.3
Independent	8.1	5.3
Conservative	1.2	0.0
No Answer	0.4	4.0

the responses to the question of shifting party allegiance: less than 6 percent of all respondents have ever switched from the Republican to the Democratic party or vice versa. Nearly 77 percent have been lifelong supporters of the same party. Moreover, our analysis of the black vote in the 1968 presidential election confirms the black Democratic preference, a point restated continually in the voting studies literature. Humphrey received 43 percent, against Nixon's 19 percent, of the Model Cities black elderly vote. The two candidates each garnered about 37 percent of the white elderly vote. But these national and state elections have not resulted in a material improvement of the welfare of the ,elderly. Increases in social security benefits contribute little to the marked improvement of the elderly poor's welfare since welfare payments are deductible from social security benefits; additionally, many elderly poor do not qualify for the maximum social security payment because of smaller contributions during their working years. The Democratic party will probably continue to take the black vote, both young and old, for granted, while the Republicans will strive to maintain their support among white voters. Political affiliation is thus not likely to become a successful rallying base for social action by the aged.

Though we do not report the figures here, education increases the extent of political participation, as it did political knowledge, shown before. In each case, those with no more than elementary education participate less than those with greater education. But from the standpoint of the advocate, the well-educated elderly poor are too few to institute an effective political lobby. Small wonder the elderly poor have little political clout.

Since this is a book about aging, we examined what effect, if any, advancing age has upon political knowledge, interest, and participation. The results are not conclusive, and vary from question to question. Only that fifth of the sample over seventy-five years of age show a consistent pattern of political disengagement. Although the very oldest show little interest and minimal participation, others from age fifty-five to seventy-five reveal few differences with advancing age. One cannot predict either the attitudinal or behavioral component of the politics of the elderly poor from a knowledge of their age, except to say that those over seventy-five withdrew on all dimensions, the oldest group containing virtually no black persons.

Summary

Advancing age is seen to have little impact on the political life of the aged poor. To be black or well-educated increases the levels of knowledge and participation, but this group is too small to sustain an effective political movement. The plain facts are that the bulk of the elderly poor display little interest in politics, make decisions on the basis of grossly inadequate information, and, apart from voting, generally abstain from political activity. Coupled with the expressed aversion to collective activity, especially the white hostility to any form of concerted action with blacks (see Chapter 4), these results are indeed bleak. The prospects for successful self-advocacy among the elderly poor are not glowing!

6 Disengagement: What Went Wrong?

This study set out to identify the wants of the elderly poor and their potential for self-advocacy. We have described their wants and, as the next chapter shows, question their capacity for successful advocacy. But we must first dispose of a fundamental question that dominates research on the elderly: does aging correlate with physical and emotional withdrawal from the pursuit of basic personal wants? This question directly confronts the theme of disengagement, a thesis for which we found virtually no support in our own study.

What went wrong with the disengagement thesis? For nearly a decade since the disengagement thesis was so convincingly put forward in *Growing Old*,[1] most gerontologists have applied this concept, in some manner, to their studies. Some believed they had confirmed the truths of "disengagement"; others questioned them with equal zeal. A body of empirical work grew on the foundation of disengagement as a generation of multidisciplinary gerontologists contended with *Growing Old*.

Cumming and Henry constructed the disengagement theory with the initial assertion that death is universal and inevitable. The next claim asserted that *both* society and the individual must therefore adjust themselves to this fact to avoid social disruption and disequilibrium in order to maintain homeostasis in the social system. That is, continued social stability and individual mental well-being required each old person to recognize the social effects of his advancing age and to adjust his social behavior and expectations accordingly. Society, as well, must recognize the decreasing importance of each of its aging elderly citizens, and reflect that awareness in its social institutions and practices. Both society and the individual prepare for this ultimate fact through the mechanism of gradual and *mutual* disengagement, a disengagement that is completed at death. The thesis of the process of disengagement posits that an individual's death, if unprepared for, is dysfunctional for the social system, and hence a functional way of preparing for death is to disengage.

Cumming and Henry inspired a decade-long debate that alternately embellished or criticized "disengagement." (Recall our review of this debate from Chapter 1.) Some distinctions were sought between voluntary and involuntary withdrawal and the concomitant effect on morale and attitudes; the disillusion of increasing age was shown to encourage the elderly to seek an accommodation with reality. Perhaps the correlates of increased physical and social stress that accompany advancing age, rather than age itself, produce disengagement. A more conservative view claims disengagement as *one*, though not the only, successful route towards adjustment in old age. That retrenchment occurs in one sphere of life need not signal complete withdrawal in all spheres.

This chapter first examines the logical structure of the Cumming and Henry thesis, which, in turn, rests on a Parsonian framework of functional analysis. A second consideration is the application of the various disengagement measures that have been constructed to our survey respondents—we undertook specifically to try to replicate the items that comprise scales of disengagement. A final search for relationships using factor analysis on those items that underlie the notion of disengagement concludes our evaluation of the concept. We believe that the disengagement thesis is inappropriate as a way to describe the urban elderly poor.

The disengagement thesis states that both society and the individual must adjust themselves to the fact that death is universal and inevitable if the social system is to be maintained in a homeostatic state. Several problems arise with this formulation. First, social systems do in fact change. The disengagement advocate postulates a nonchanging world and the fact of social change may be entirely independent of aging and its inevitable culmination in death. Everyone must die, in both social systems that suffer cataclysmic upheaval or those which remain in a homeostatic state. Secondly, some people may refuse to recognize that death is inevitable. They die nonetheless, and society is not generally disrupted by their maladjustment to the fact of death. Thirdly, the disengagement thesis is couched in a form that precludes disconfirmation on the basis of real world observation, a necessary condition of scientific assertion. How do we determine if a disruption in the social system is due to old people refusing to accept their inevitable death and that because they are maladjusted they disrupt an otherwise homeostatic social system? The logic of disengagement is tautological—there is no way to disprove or falsify it. It cannot, therefore, qualify as a theory to be used in scientific accounts of the process of aging. What difference does it make to the continued existence of society if an individual fails to adjust to his impending death? It only makes a difference to the individual in question—and he is going to die anyway—and probably has no effect on the continued existence or stability of the society. If a given society disintegrates—which the failure of individuals to adjust to their impending deaths should bring about—how do we prove that social chaos is due to recalcitrance among the aged or a dozen such other factors as conquest, war, famine, corruption, etc.?

There is thus no way to prove or disprove the thesis: social disruption may be due to a variety of factors that need not include the failure of the aged to adjust to the realization of death; furthermore, social stability may continue even if the aged do not adjust—especially since these persons by definition become inefficacious, inarticulate, and increasingly dependent on the rest of society. The very fact of this growing inefficiency and loss of articulateness more likely make the older person irrelevant to society. It makes little difference whether he withdraws or not.

An Empirical Test of Disengagement[2]

The notion of disengagement is multidimensional: it includes the psychological, physical, economic, and political. To disengage suggests that with advancing age, older persons experience a constriction of life space, which might be reflected in such terms or behavior as alienation, dissatisfaction with life, withdrawal from social activities, a recognition of the need for reduced activities, and perhaps increasing willingness to acknowledge the problems of the young as having greater priority. The questionnaire (see Appendix A) reveals the extent to which we posed the question of disengagement in surveying the urban elderly poor. More than any other concept, the thesis of disengagement governed the construction of the interview schedule. We are therefore able to dissect its multidimensional character for the Model Cities' aged in Rochester.

The psychological dimension appears in Table 6-1. We segregated respondents into successive five-year age categories which are, of course, cross-sectional in nature. We do not have data that bear

Table 6-1
Psychological Disengagement by Age Group (by percentages)

Item	(N=67) 55-59	(N=60) 60-64	(N=75) 65-69	(N=60) 70-74	(N=70) 75+
Do people care about helping others? (affirmative response)	73.1	60.0	68.0	65.0	71.4
Do people have fewer cares after retirement?	50.7	36.7	53.3	45.0	47.1
Should the old retire to make room for the young?	74.6	68.3	77.3	65.0	70.0
Do the old share common problems?	53.7	58.3	56.0	65.0	54.3
Can old people solve common problems by working together?	65.7	71.7	74.7	70.0	60.0

directly upon the changes in behavior or attitudes people undergo as they age, but instead are forced to make inferences about the chronological processes of aging from a static analysis of successive five-year groups of the aged who display a comparable social and economic life style for each race. It could be, of course, that differences between age categories are attributable to sequential environmental changes or to other capricious effects. Recall, however, that a substantial portion of these elderly, especially the whites, have lived in the same area, indeed the same house, for several decades, which suggests that cross-sectional analysis for this community of aged is relatively risk-free of substantial environmental variation.

Note the affirmative response to the first entry in Table 6-1: Do people care about helping others? Personal cynicism is highest within the sixty to sixty-four age group, which suffers from rapid economic retrenchment (see Chapter 2). Otherwise, no significant differences emerge among age groups—indeed, those over seventy-five years of age have a view of human nature at least as attractive as their younger counterparts.

Do people have fewer cares after retirement? Should the old retire to make room for the young? Do the old share common problems? Can the old solve common problems by working together? The responses by age group to each of these questions challenges, even belies, the assertion of gradual, continuous disengagement. Advancing age does not induce a fundamental constriction of psychological life space. Evidently, the old do not change their view of human nature and aging to reflect the reality of their aging.

Thus, if our measures are meaningful, no visible psychological disengagement has taken place among the elderly poor in our sample. What about the physical correlates of advancing age? Employment, as noted before, diminishes with age: 47.8 percent in the fifty-five to fifty-nine group work full time, but only 28.3 percent are similarly employed in the next category. Over sixty-five, only a trivial number of the elderly remain employed full time. This decline is undoubtedly due to limited employment opportunities and the availability of social security for those over sixty-five. An examination of two other forms of social activity, membership in social clubs and visiting of friends, turns up no discernible pattern of disengagement. Note in Table 6-2 that membership in social clubs varies unpredictably with age—the fifth bracket is not significantly less active, statistically, than the second. As well, age has no seeming impact on the frequency of seeing friends on a regular basis.

Table 6-2
Social Activity Disengagement by Age Group (by percentages)

Item	(N=67) 55-59	(N=60) 60-64	(N=75) 65-69	(N=60) 70-74	(N=70) 75+
Social Club Membership	22.4	18.3	28.0	23.3	14.3
See Friends Weekly	61.2	60.0	61.3	55.0	58.6

One area in which increasing age bears upon the elderly poor is in their physical mobility. Table 6-3 reveals a pronounced pattern of reduced mobility. With few exceptions, progressively higher percentages of persons report physical mobility difficulty with advancing age. However, reduced mobility does not correlate with constrictions

Table 6-3
Mobility by Age Group (by percentages)

Item	(N=67) 55-59	(N=60) 60-64	(N=75) 65-69	(N=60) 70-74	(N=70) 75+
Hard to go up and down stairs	26.9	35.0	40.0	41.7	52.9
Hard to leave building	9.0	16.7	21.3	26.7	41.4
Hard to go shopping	19.4	21.7	29.3	28.3	38.6
Hard to get into and out of bed	6.0	8.3	26.7	16.7	38.6
Hard to walk around the room	7.5	5.0	14.7	18.3	28.6

in psychological life space—indeed, our evidence questions if there is any connection at all between the two. Although age inhibits physical mobility it does not reduce psychological well-being.

We also explored the political dimension of disengagement, both in terms of attitudes and reported behavior, specifically the effects of advancing age upon political knowledge, political efficacy, citizen duty, and reported participation. Table 6-4 captures the attitudinal

Table 6-4
Political Disengagement (Attitudinal) by Age Group (by percentages)

Item	(N=67) 55-59	(N=60) 60-64	(N=75) 65-69	(N=60) 70-74	(N=70) 75+
Should not vote if your party doesn't have a chance to win	32.8 (67.2)*	18.3 (81.7)	26.7 (73.3)	33.3 (66.7)	22.9 (77.1)
Should not vote if you don't care how the election comes out	56.7 (43.4)	43.3 (56.7)	50.7 (49.3)	51.7 (48.3)	37.1 (62.9)
Public officials don't care about what old people think	43.3	46.7	56.0	56.7	52.9
Politics is too complicated for old people to understand	82.1	80.0	84.0	81.7	91.4
Correctly identify Model Cities	17.9	18.3	18.7	15.0	5.7
Have heard of Model Cities, but not correctly identify	37.3	35.0	22.7	23.3	32.9

*Number in parentheses indicates percentage giving opposite reply, i.e., disagreeing with the statement.

component of politics. Note first that those over seventy-five are most committed to the importance of the voting act in and of itself, even in the absence of election interest or likely victory for one's preferred party (the first two items in Table 6-4). This result flatly contradicts the notion of withdrawal—on the contrary, commitment reaches a peak for those most enfeebled by old age. This is not compatible with the Cumming and Henry thesis. Note further that no discernible patterns of gradual and continuous disengagement characterize this community of elderly—only the very oldest may be more cynical, frustrated, or less well-informed than the youngest, but no pattern of steady withdrawal appears. Finally, from Table 6-5, those over seventy-five show a reduction in actual participation or interest in joining a community action group. But, if these findings are nationally typical, then the age at which disengagement begins should be revised upwards to seventy-five and over.

Table 6-5
Political Disengagement (Behavior) by Age Group (by percentages)

Item	(N=67) 55-59	(N=60) 60-64	(N=75) 65-69	(N=60) 70-74	(N=70) 75+
Vote in 1970	68.7	78.3	72.0	61.7	55.7
Donate money to candidates	17.9	13.3	9.3	10.0	2.9
Discuss politics with others	13.4	11.7	10.7	6.7	4.3
Interested in community action group	38.8	33.3	33.3	30.0	14.3

Each of the items discussed in this chapter, along with numerous others obtained from the interviews, was entered into a factor analysis in the hope that we might locate some underlying dimension which captured the notion of disengagement. We juxtaposed the entire collection of disengagement items against ten major factors which emerged from the analysis. Age loaded only on the factors of physical mobility and retirement—as our discussion has earlier disclosed. Elsewhere it had no impact. Indeed, the analysis disclosed no underlying dimension attributable to chronological age.[3] Thus, a logical critique, cross-sectional comparisons, and the failure of factor analysis to locate common dimensions suggest that the concept of disengagement be abandoned, a recommendation that has recently received loud support. Gisela Labouvie points to this same conclusion:

Recognition of the need for a re-orientation of descriptive research in intellectual ontogeny is stimulated by two circumstances. First, the finding of significant cohort differences demonstrated that there was minimal justification for the long-lived assumption of behavioral deficit in the elderly. Instead, it became necessary to assume that cross-sectional differences between young and old subjects primarily reflect nondevelopmental (i.e., generational) differences, thus suggesting that behavior is continually monitored by environmental parameters. Second, it became obvious that age-performance functions possessed little generality, but it required a more and more elaborate breakdown into differential curves according to such parameters as ability domain, cohort membership, and even subgroups within cohorts (e.g., ability level, educational status, health status.) As a consequence, *the notion of differential age functions now has reached such a state of indeterminacy as to be of no predictive value whatsoever.* Similar arguments, parenthetically apply with equal force to other areas of development. As an example, recent assessments of disengagement theory suggest a comparable state of confusion as to what life circumstances are reliably linked with specific adaptational outcomes.[4] (emphasis added)

Professor Labouvie presented her conclusions in a panel devoted to the topic of psychogerontology—the psychological factors associated with aging. Commenting on that paper, Professor Schaie expressed an even stronger conviction that the disengagement concept be abandoned.

... But I will go a step further to show that the concept of *chronological age,* except as used by the actuarian and demographer, *is not only useless but indeed a dangerous concept* in the treatment of developmental phenomena which occur after the species-specific adult (mature) level has been attained.[5] (emphasis added)

Thus, in conceptualizing the political and social efficacy of the elderly—a major topic of this book—the "cornerstone" of disengagement would be a millstone. We chose, instead, to study the preferences and choices of our subjects, for which they retain a capacity to the most advanced age, even for those who are poor.

7

Advocacy by the Aged [a]

What is the potential of self-advocacy among the aged poor to improve their material or psychological conditions? This study created a group—albeit exclusively white—in order to evaluate the promise of self-advocacy. Indeed, we might construe the creation of an advocacy group of aged poor as an exogenous given for the purposes of this study. The research and demonstration project that this book reports called explicitly for the creation of an advocacy group of elderly poor and the study of those conditions under which it would evolve and succeed or fail.

With *Maximum Feasible Misunderstanding* creating a brouhaha over needless and misguided external intervention by government or government-supported professionals, we sought to design a very careful, and very limited, strategy for intervention into the community. Critical in this design was the development and training of a low-profile community organizer that would not impose his or her expertise and leadership over the organization so formed; otherwise, the purpose of the entire project would be defeated and we would have no answer as to whether the elderly could effectively organize themselves for social action roles. As part of the strategy we searched for and evaluated the experiences of those elsewhere who had claimed experience in organizing the elderly for social action, from the widely acclaimed "Council on Elders" in Massachusetts,[1] which we quickly recognized as really advocacy by professionals in the name of the aged, to others scattered throughout the United States that were, in the main, also advocacy groups surrogated by professionals.[2] We were unable to locate an effort directly comparable with our assigned task of helping form, and then minimally intervene in the affairs of, a self-advocacy group of the elderly poor.

The starting point was, of course, the survey in which respondents were asked if they had any interest in joining a community action group of older citizens in the neighborhood—a group that gets

[a]This chapter was prepared with the assistance of Gloria M. Gioia.

61

together to solve common problems. The community organizer almost immediately approached these persons about the possibility of a preliminary meeting and met with universal resistance. Even that bare minority of interested respondents did not convert their reported interest into behavioral interest. But we are somewhat ahead of the story at this point.

Perhaps the best way to tell the story of social advocacy by the elderly in Rochester's Model Cities is in the words of our young, twenty-two-year-old community organizer, a carefully selected low-key individual (female) with university training in gerontological studies, and a deep personal interest in the well-being of elderly persons.

In order to get a feel for the area, I repeatedly walked throughout the entire Model Cities Area. I chose a target area for community organization after having identified existing senior citizens' groups, and the pertinent agencies that serve older clients. The area chosen lies in the northwest section of Model Cities directly above the Upper Falls Urban Renewal Project (an area still containing a relatively substantial white population). I entered the area in the fall of 1971, generally looked for persons outdoors to speak with, and engaged a number of people relaxing in their yards and several neighborhood shopkeepers. I was determined to keep my priorities clear: the objective of the project is to determine whether the elderly poor could organize for social action purposes. The key question in my mind was, and still is, what minimum level of support do they require for success?

After conversing with a number of persons repeatedly in their yards, or on their front porches, I was often invited in for coffee and cookies. Contacts of this sort soon led to other introductions, invariably situated about the kitchen table. (It has been a constant struggle to keep my weight down for the past two years.)

On the basis of these contacts, I hopefully set about a first neighborhood meeting in November 1971, but was disappointed when not a single elderly person arrived. In my own defense I reasoned that a 5 inch snowstorm had conspired against me, but also that I had not perhaps made the right set of contacts. People often readily agree to attend such meetings (an easy answer) simply because it is easier to say yes than to say no, an aspect of human nature.

I returned, though, to walking and talking, on different days, at different times of the day, finally settling upon mid-afternoon as the best time to catch my target community. Mid-afternoon seems, for them, the best time for shopping and yard work. The elderly women were then often easily reachable in the early afternoon as they would be at home watching the serialized television programs. We had many helpful conversations during the commercials (I really saw a good deal of afternoon television in the early going) and often they would turn off the program to sit and chat with me.

One woman proved to be especially interested in what I was doing. I soon stopped in to visit with her about once every week. By chance she mentioned that her husband was retiring and would be taking over the business that she had run for the past twenty years. She had not yet decided what next she might do and seemed virtually perfect as an aide for my community organization work. In March 1972 I hired her, then trained her and sent her out walking and talking in the target neighborhood.

A curious feature of attempting community organization was that I soon found myself in amateur social work. I helped obtain meals on wheels for two interested older persons. Yet another lady met the field aide through her grocer, a local independent, who sent the aide over to see if the lady was interested in meals-on-wheels. The field aide then heard a description of all her difficulties: bills had not been paid in months, the electricity was going to be turned off, the telephone had already been disconnected, no city or county taxes had been paid. We managed to get several of these bills paid and arranged for a professional social worker to step in. The lady is now a client of a family service agency. The social worker handling her case recently said to me "that client will be the death of me." A guardian has now been appointed to see that all bills are paid, but she has rejected all further overtures of assistance.

As my relationship built up with several of the older persons in the area, our conversations shifted tone. In the beginning I heard chiefly about neighborhood problems that had been caused by the in-migration of blacks and Puerto Ricans, or about their aches and pains. One lady remarked that "Many blacks and Puerto Ricans are moving in—some are nice, but most are bad." Another said that he "Doesn't like Model Cities Program—that it is mostly for blacks." One older home owner remarked that "There's no point in fixing one's home, because those around yours are getting worse, so you'll never be able to get your money out." More significant were the comments of one older person: "Our neighborhood is bad since they (Puerto Ricans and blacks) all moved in. All we have now are groups of people on front porches all day with the record player blaring, drinking beer, and the roaring of cars down the street. We never thought we would live with them when we moved here." One terrified person expressed the view that "You cannot always or continually keep calling police—they might retaliate if they thought you were the one who called the police."

Later conversations discussed several of the aged's general life philosophy, how they feel about life and death. I found myself doing a lot of listening and was initially disturbed when the conversations shifted to talk of death.

Early home visits lasted about 30 to 45 minutes and now they invariably run from one to two hours. Indeed, it is getting harder and harder to get out of one home and onto a visit to the next. I am constantly forced to eat three pieces of cake every afternoon and drink four to six cups of coffee. People get upset when for some reason I can't manage to eat all they want me to or think I should.

I've also felt it only right or fair to tell these elderly persons what I am doing when they have asked. The thing they are most concerned about is that I should be married and I have had countless offers of introductions to grandsons, through matrimonial matches have been less important to them after the first year.

The neighborhood has changed in many ways since I began working. When I first walked through the neighborhood in March 1971, the area was quiet, houses and yards were in generally good repair, and a large number of senior citizens lived in the area. I returned to the field again in the fall of 1971 and perceived no major physical or sociological changes. During the winter I began to notice changes in the race and age structure of the population. The streets were not so well plowed and the snow was littered with paper and garbage. By the spring of 1972 there were substantially more black families, and a great increase in the number of Spanish-speaking families, with many children and teenagers playing in the street. Many houses were now up for sale and the yards were poorly maintained. Loud music and poor property maintenance became a frequent topic of conversation throughout the summer.

My first meeting in November 1971 produced exactly a zero attendance. By May of 1972 I was now brave enough, with the help of my trained aide from that spring, to try again. None of the attendees came from the survey respondents who said they were interested in forming a community action group of elderly. Rather, they were all people who had been carefully cultivated for many months. In other words, a very lasting and deep relationship had first to be built up between me and them before they were willing to commit themselves to any kind of meeting. I felt delightedly proud when six senior citizens arrived to inaugurate the group. Among those one said she viewed the group as a chance to make new friends, another wanted to be in on the ground floor, and yet another sought neighborhood improvement. As was true then, and still now, the overwhelming majority of group regulars were elderly ladies in their very late sixties or early to mid-seventies. I would guess the average age of the group to be in the low seventies. In the regular membership is one lady who requires a cane, another who uses a crutch, one with a special cane, several who are hard of hearing, and several receiving old age assistance. All were members of Senior Citizens Action Council before joining the group.

This first successful meeting in May was devoted to discussing the objectives and directions of such a group, followed by a consideration of possible meeting topics: neighborhood problems, youth, public transportation, and problems peculiar to the elderly.

The third meeting, though second in terms of some attendance, witnessed twelve participants and lasted over two hours. Each person first introduced himself and then the group discussed what people consider to be problems for which help might be sought from professionals. The group also discussed the philosophy of group action for community betterment.

A would be fourth meeting in mid-July had to be cancelled due to an intense heat wave in which the senior citizens did not want to venture out. A week later, it was held in the basement of a local church, which has since become the regular meeting site, but only four members turned out. Still the session had a guest speaker from outside Model Cities and the meeting lasted for three hours. The subsequent August meeting only turned out five persons. Although a core of four senior citizens had now formed, a successful advocacy group would obviously require substantially more neighborhood participation and I was becoming concerned about my own possible failures as an unobtrusive community organizer.

I resisted the temptation to take a more active role in directing my group of elderly citizens, knowing full well that such increased tempo would violate the spirit and point of the entire project: could the elderly form their own self-advocacy group? Fortunately, the next month broke the dry spell and the sixth meeting in September 1972 saw a turnout of seven. The meeting lasted about three hours and the chief topic of discussion was how to expand with new members. It was suggested that a luncheon be held for the next session. Meanwhile, several of the group members began to accompany me on an individual basis to various planning meetings on the arts, and informative meetings for senior citizens.

I think it important to bear in mind that I did not run these meetings. In fact, I should best be described as a quiet bystander, and only spoke or replied when specifically asked for information. Otherwise, the elderly managed their own meetings.

The planned luncheon achieved a primary goal: membership expanded to ten, of whom six were new persons. The most important event in the entire history of the group (from November's abortive effort through May 1973) occurred during the lunch meeting in which it was decided that a police department representative should be the guest speaker at the following November 1972 meeting.

Attendance shot up dramatically to seventeen, and thereafter the group held steady in size from seventeen to about twenty. From working with these elderly one thing became particularly clear: a concern for personal safety on the streets of their neighborhood. By having the Chief of Detectives come to speak, it signalled to the group that there might be some genuine community concern for their wants. As one elderly man had put it: "When I walk down the street and see kids roaming around in a group arm-in-arm, I go directly into my house. I'm an old man and can no longer defend myself." Another man noted that "I hire several neighborhood kids to watch my house when both my wife and I go out."

Indeed, so impressive was the police spokesman, that many elderly wished to have such a representative return repeatedly to future meetings. This meeting gave the group a chance to talk about purse snatchings, house break-ins, and other safety concerns. One member presented the chief with a written statement. The meeting was concluded by deciding to invite a speaker from Social Security for the next session.

Thereafter, the meetings averaged near twenty senior citizens each, and often included a show and tell session in which persons brought in crafts in which they worked: knitting, crocheting, wooden candlesticks, table-top decorations. At times films were obtained and shown, several members attended a spring dance and luncheon for senior citizens sponsored by a local senior citizens organization, and various excursions were arranged for such visits as the planetarium, picnics, etc.

Although I often provided first-hand information about programs and changes that affect senior citizens such as the establishment of a County Office for Aging, changes in medical assistance for senior citizens, and so forth, the group has not yet formulated any definite program of social action. Hearing about existing programs and program changes did not engender any militant movements for demanding more social services from the community. Films, recreations, picnics, luncheons, and personal activities seemed always to be uppermost in their minds.

I retired from my official position as paid community organizer in May 1973, but promised the group that I would continue on an unpaid basis, and that I would most likely venture into other activities that involved programs and elderly activities. My job was, obviously, extremely satisfying and I derived a good deal of "utility" in working with these older people; they, as well, seemed to enjoy having me work with them. One lady, who had given up going to church, made group meetings her only outings from her home.

My views on the success potential of elderly advocacy? Based upon several years of forming, working with, and avoiding giving anything more than a bare minimum of direction and guidance, I suspect that social activities will continue to provide the meaning and basis for group persistence for each of these elderly citizens. I simply cannot see how they can become an effective political force without substantial external direction and resources. My observations of other groups confirm this belief. The remaining groups of old people in Model Cities seem to be dictated to by the group professional director; they rubber stamp suggestions for programs and activities by the professional director, and attend meetings only because things are given to them that provide some element of personal utility. But these groups do not seem internally well-motivated and might fold without external direction. I am wishful that mine will not. Effective social action, in my view, will require professional surrogate activity; the concept of self-advocacy among the urban elderly poor is inappropriate and unrealistic.

At one meeting, I suggested that we consider joining forces with an already established black group of senior citizens. The proposal met with *universal* resistance and hostility and I thereafter determined that even to raise the topic might lead to the disbanding of the group if they felt that racial integration was one of my purposes.

In retrospect, one of the most important factors in the formation and maintenance of my group was my car. It first allowed me flexibility in scheduling of home visiting and neighborhood observation. It also now constitutes a limitation on my freedom: my elderly group members see the car and immediately chastise me for not having stopped to visit with them, even when I had other appointments scheduled. But perhaps more important is the fact that my car enabled several members to attend meetings who would otherwise not be able to attend. During the last few months of my task, the church at which the group regularly meets provided a mini-bus and the transportation requirement, for the moment, seems under control. It was, however, in my opinion most crucial.

We have let the community organizer tell her own story. Her personal success in forming a group that did not thereafter require her daily direction (transportation notwithstanding) differentiated her from most of the other groups we observed in the Rochester Model Cities area and also from those groups that we learned about from an analysis of the relevant literature. Her conclusion that social advocacy is more wishful thinking than practical possibility conforms to the analysis of social service agencies (which appears in the next chapter) and the results of our survey respondents from the beginning of the project.

On a concluding note, it is clear that concern for personal safety, as discussed in the earlier analysis and in the report of the community organizer, is not unique to Rochester. An important study by Joel Aberbach and Jack Walker of the multiracial inner city of Detroit paints a similar portrait. In the view of one of their respondents:

The neighborhood had changed profoundly during the forty years she had lived there. It had once been full of families she knew and trusted but now was inhabited by strangers; it had been all white and now was almost all black. She found this change in her environment deeply threatening; hers was a life of almost perpetual fear. She reported that during the year before our interview her purse had been stolen from her twice on the street and her house had been broken into once. . . . Her declining energies and prospects, her poverty, her unhappiness at changes taking place all around her, led to a powerful yearning for personal security. Policemen "should walk the beats. We need more police protection, instead of just driving by real fast." . . . When asked about the best possible life imaginable she said: "I would just like to live free of fear. I want to know I can walk the streets and be safe either day or night. I don't want to be scared every time the bell rings."[3]

Purse-snatching, house break-ins, the quest for personal security describe precisely the world of the urban elderly poor.

8

Serving the Elderly[1]

Assume a hypothetical world in which the urban elderly poor are organized for collective self-advocacy—they possess a coherent group preference ordering, they enthusiastically support concerted multi-racial action to improve their material and psychological well-being, and they are effectively organized with but the barest minimum of external direction, as the previous chapter has disclosed. What obstacles to obtaining its desired, agreed-upon service goals would this group of elderly poor encounter in its practice of self-advocacy? Would it meet with relatively immediate and dramatic success in the fulfillment of its subjectively-determined wants? Or, would it uncover an inchoate collage of variegated bureaus, frustrated service workers, and cynical agency directors, which, all told, seemed more likely to oppose and frustrate rather than satisfy the desires of the group? Or, would it meet with a world in between these extremes?

Although our assessment of service delivery is confined to Model Cities, we believe that our findings bear upon the more general world of the core city, especially as these services are geared to the elderly poor of white, black, or other minority group origin. The theme of this chapter is that any organized group of aged poor would, in pursuing its interests, encounter a confused, disorganized, indeed at times contradictory bundle of service organizations which may not, in themselves, possess the ability to effectively serve their target clients.

Chapter 4 revealed that the racial factor predominates in the interpersonal world of the white elderly poor. Accordingly, we examine how difference in race relates to the attitudes and behavior of service personnel as they enjoin the task of serving the elderly. Another aspect to our examination of service delivery is found in the notion of "rational man," which applies as equally to the career bureaucrat as it does to the elderly poor.

As Niskanen points out, sociologists and political scientists have almost monopolized the study of bureaucratic behavior.[2] Only three book-length economic treatments of bureaucracy exist.[3] What

71

distinguishes these economic analyses from the others, however, is their ready acceptance of the self-interest axiom of human nature that underlies most economic reasoning, and which serves as the logical base in our analysis of more than 350 Model Cities elderly. This approach, we recall, postulates that individuals are adjudged to know their own preferences, to be capable of ordering them from most-preferred to least-preferred, and to be able to make choices that provide the greatest satisfaction. Bureaucrats are *not* a special breed of altruistic animal. They, too, have personal preferences, which are often revealed in the statements and decisions they make, especially when bureaucratic outcomes differ from the stated goals of the organization.

In Niskanen's words, "As individuals, bureaucrats are neither inherently superior nor inferior, but it is unwise not to recognize that they have some differentiating characteristics."[4] Bureaus attract persons who are most likely very good at playing the game of bureaucracy, i.e., obtaining such rewards that a bureaucracy can offer to its members as pecuniary gain, promotion, advancement in status, and power over other individuals. Survival of the fittest assures that bureaucrats who get ahead probably possess these maximizing characteristics.

How does a bureau or service agency director get ahead? By pleasing (serving) his designated target clients? Or, conversely, by serving his sovereigns?—the board members who provide his funding, determine his policies, and rule on his salary and promotion. The evidence, we believe, points to the predomination of the latter mode, viz., that agency directors more assiduously cultivate the favor of their sovereigns who sit in judgment on them than they seek to satisfy the wants of their clients, in this case the elderly poor. Although disgruntled clients with clout can made the life of an agency director miserable, it is, realistically, only the influential board members who possess the clout and legal responsibility for the agency's activities, which includes the material well-being of the director. Hence, the dictates of career advancement in the bureaucratic environment may not be consistent with the pursuits of the advocacy group, unless sovereign-pleasing behavior coincides with client-pleasing behavior. There is even a strong argument to be made that the sovereigns, while interested in supporting the services the agency is supposed to provide *do not want* real information on the actual success or failure of the services. They want the agency to appear to be succeeding, to have the executive appear to carry out their goals, whether he does so or not.[5]

Three themes thus orchestrate the analysis of social service delivery: (1) agency directors are rewarded or punished on the basis of their success or failure in serving their sovereigns, and not necessarily their poor elderly clients; (2) service delivery in Rochester's inner city is disorganized and somewhat inchoate—any advocacy group of the aged would have a difficult time in discerning an efficacious course of action; and (3) there is a racial dimension to service delivery that, given the importance of the racial variable, may impinge upon successful group advocacy. The prospects of successful advocacy in this environment are bleak; our proposals in the next chapter constitute, of necessity, a departure from the traditions of conventional service delivery to the *needy*.

Research Procedures

A careful review of those agencies that provide community services to the elderly poor in Model Cities led us to contact for interview twenty-two agency directors.[a] This list of agencies was compiled on the cumulative basis of knowledge acquired by project members of several years of working or living in the Model Cities area, including those persons hired from within the area to work on the staff. We identified those agencies in the area that might serve the elderly if they were not already doing so, and also those agencies serving the entire city, county, or region that could be of possible help to the elderly in the Model Cities area. These would comprise the potential targets for advocacy. Direct service delivery to the elderly varies, of course, in degree and scope from agency to agency, from an exclusive focus on the aged to, at best, a tangential concern. Each director participated in a structured, though heavily open-end, interview session that lasted upwards of an hour (see Appendix B for this interview schedule).

It would have been ideal to interview a random sample of board and staff members in these twenty-two agencies—those persons who

---

[a]See Appendix C for the list of selected agencies. Because we are not dealing either with personalities or specific agencies in this chapter, and because anonymity is essential, specific agency responses are not identified. We talk only in the more important aggregate terms.

help formulate and carry out agency programs and policies. Completion of this strategy would permit the directors' responses to be compared with those of his board and staff and thereby constitute a test of the Niskanen model bureaucrat. Unfortunately, this was impossible.

During the time of our agency interviews, the Community Chest was undergoing a major reorganization. Our own agency to which this project was attached, the Citizens Planning Council, was itself subsequently merged into an enlarged Community Chest. The Model Cities program was also under considerable stress, and many of the agencies we sought to study were either Chest-related or partially funded by Model Cities. Many agencies were also threatened by city-wide and county-wide financial cutbacks. The environment was not conducive to straightforward investigation and many persons were suspicious of our intentions. Although each of the fifteen board members we ultimately interviewed was either the president or chairman of his board (or stand-in), we were unable to obtain a random selection of staff members.

In a less hostile research environment we would have approached each agency for an organization chart of its personnel and then have randomly selected from a list those staff members whose functions were most closely related to possible programs for the elderly. To have in fact made that request would, in our opinion, have evoked flat rejection of any interviews in many agencies. One director, for example, whose agency is clearly noncontroversial, called our office six times to find out why the survey was being conducted, and expressed great anxiety over possible use of the material against his agency. Another director refused permission to interview any of his staff, falsely declaring he had none. Yet another refused permission to interview a member of his board: In every case initial contact was made with the director and he or she, when willing, made arrangements for interviews with hand-picked board and staff members. The director thus had the opportunity to keep us from talking with staff members whose views he opposed.

One final point. Throughout the three years of the project, attempts were often made to influence or control the use of our funds, even to the point of threatening the advocacy group we helped form. In order to protect the project's interests we could not, as a Chest-related agency, appear to be threatening the activities of other Chest agencies. This necessitated a low profile, albeit resulting in an admittedly nonrandom sample. Nonetheless, the results are interesting in their own right.

To augment the information collected during the interviews, we examined the purposes, goals, and actual operating programs as published in the official statements of the agencies. Finally, we talked with a select number of well-informed persons in the community who were able to provide insight into the origin of Model Cities and its various programs and who could evaluate the agencies that, taken together, comprise the present system of service delivery. These latter interviews are not arrayed in tabular form but were instead used to inform the more objective statistical analyses of the agency interviews.

Our sample was thus restricted to about sixty respondents, a number too small to permit much cross-tabulational analysis. Accordingly, only those distributions that meet the standard of statistical significance at the .05 level appear in tabular form. Other results were obtained by regression analysis; its more robust technique permits the discovery of statistically significant results with a much smaller number of observations.

An Overview of Agency Actors

As but three respondents are Puerto Rican, our discussion focuses upon the thirty-six white and twenty-one black agency personnel. By position, respondents of each race are about equally well-represented. Table 8-1 shows that near similar percentages of each race staff the positions of director, board member, and staff worker. This result may be partly an artifact of the selection process by which board and staff members were designated for interview. The point of the table, though, is to show that race does not correlate with position and that members of each race do varied tasks on behalf of the agencies.

Race differentiates the scope and nature of service delivery. Among black respondents, 76 percent claim that the scope of their agency's activities is confined to Model Cities and other portions of what may be termed the inner city. Whites, by contrast, report an analogous figure of just over 30 percent. Conversely, almost 70 percent of the latter (the white personnel) see their agency in a city-wide or county-wide role. Thus black and white agents serve

Table 8-1
Position Within Agency by Race

Position	(N=36) Whites	(N=21) Blacks
Board Member	22.2	28.6
Director	38.9	33.3
Staff Member	38.9	38.1

different clientele. Given a relatively high concentration of blacks in the inner city (including Model Cities), we might expect to encounter black service specialists who could perhaps better resolve the specified wants of the black clients. Might this create the possibility that the white elderly poor would increasingly have to seek services from black-staffed organizations in their neighborhood? Racial antipathies revealed earlier suggest that white clients will suffer psychological costs in pursuit of material assistance if forced to deal with non-white agencies.

For the moment, as Table 8-2 indicates, elderly whites deal chiefly with white-staffed agencies. Note from the table that nearly one-fourth of all blacks—board members, directors, and staff workers—do not identify with agencies that serve the elderly. Indeed, no black works for the exclusive behalf of the elderly. Serving the elderly, at present, is predominately a white service activity.

Respondents were also asked to specify the future orientation and programs of their respective agencies, especially as they pertained to the elderly. Among whites, 39 percent see future programs oriented toward the elderly; for blacks, less than 15 percent. Hence, in the immediate future, whites will, in all likelihood, continue to serve both blacks and whites among the Model Cities elderly poor.

The Racial Variant

Several questions sought to assess how the service agents perceived the relationship of their agency to the target clients. When asked about satisfaction with clients' understanding of the operations of their agencies, 76 percent of the blacks, compared with 36 percent among whites, responded in the affirmative. Proportionately five times as many whites were dissatisfied with their clients' understanding of agency programs.

Table 8-2
Agency Orientation

	(N=36) Whites	(N=21) Blacks
Elderly Alone	27.8	0.0
Elderly and Others	5.6	19.0
All Ages	44.4	47.6
No Elderly	11.1	23.8
No Clients*	8.3	4.8
Don't Know	2.8	4.8

*Several of the agencies are engaged in broad planning or social change advocacy activities and, hence, do not directly deal with clients.

Should staff members act in the interests of clients if such action counters the official goals and purposes of the agency? Four-fifths of the blacks take the side of the client against only two-fifths among whites. By a ratio of two to one, blacks believe the welfare of the client precedes the welfare of the service organization. What about client receptivity to the efforts of the agency? All but one of the blacks believe their clients to be receptive; fully one-third of the whites accuse their clients of nonreceptivity. Blacks evince a more humane bond to the clients they serve; whites are more aloof, more disgruntled, and more concerned with the vested interests of their organizations. A marginally higher (but statistically significant) 86 percent of blacks, compared with 72 percent among whites, are satisfied with the policies of their agencies. As anticipated, blacks report that they serve chiefly black clients. Elderly whites in Model Cities do not, therefore, confront an encouraging service environment. Though they might receive better treatment at the hands of blacks, they are not likely to make such overtures.

A Portrait of the Director

In this section we compare the responses of the directors of those twenty-two agencies that we determined bear upon potential service opportunities for the elderly poor with those of board and staff members. Underlying our assessment of the directorship is the Niskanen model of the "rational" bureaucrat, i.e., the director who seeks to maximize his own personal utility. Our working assumption is that the director is first and foremost concerned with the impression he creates for board members, who determine career mobility.

Note first from Table 8-3 that directors, more than either staff or

Table 8-3
Are the Wants of the Elderly Being Met in Rochester?

	(N=15) Board Member	(N=22) Director	(N=23) Staff Member
Successfully	0.0	4.5	8.7
Somewhat Successfully	26.7	54.5	26.1
Somewhat Unsuccessfully	26.7	27.3	30.4
Unsuccessfully	46.7	13.6	34.8

board members, believe the wants of the elderly in Rochester are being successfully met. Agency directors are more optimistic than board and staff members. They are, at the same time, more resistant to change: 40 percent oppose program changes compared with 13 percent among the board and 17 percent within the staff. Intertwined with an optimistic account of the present system of service delivery for the elderly is a greater degree of disenchantment with the expressed wants of their clients. Twenty-seven percent of the directors reflect dissatisfaction with client wants compared to 13 percent among board and staff. Directors, in short, are less enamored of clients than board or staff. We should note that they do not deal as directly with clients as staff members. Clients may, therefore, represent for the director a source of irritation and not a source of satisfaction.

Each respondent was also asked if he (or she) were satisfied with his career or involvement in social services. None of the board members expressed dissatisfaction, only one of the staff members replied in the negative, but, significantly, over one-quarter of the directors stated that their personal dissatisfaction with a career in service delivery. In short, directors portray outward optimism, inward hostility to change, disenchantment with clients, and some dissatisfaction with their own career choice. This depiction does not describe a present or a future of efficient and concerned service delivery to the elderly.

The Niskanen effect shows up more concretely in replies to questions relating directors with their board.[b] The model predicts

---

[b]The regressions on which the next three paragraphs are based appear in Appendix D.

that directors will speak favorably and enthusiastically about the board, which sits in authority over the director's career. Public displeasure with one's boss is not conducive to career mobility. For example, directors describe the boards of their agencies as receptive and cooperative. As a group, they depict board members as receptive to program change, unlike staff members who consider the board unreceptive to program change. Does the board, with ultimate responsibility for the agency's activities, understand the operating problems of the agency? Directors say yes. As well, they ascribe to the board the responsibility for funding new and existing programs, not the design of new programs, while corresponding staff members believe the boards generally unwilling to fund new programs.

Is the agency considered successful by its chief actors? Consistent with the optimistic image previously portrayed by directors, they assert most strongly that their agencies have a positive impact on the lives of Rochester's elderly poor. The most dramatic evidence of the Niskanen effect is seen in response to that question which elicited opinions on the formation of new programs. Directors clearly want new programs to be implemented through their own agencies as opposed to joint ventures with other neighborhood agencies.

This characterization of the agency director reveals a person patently concerned with his or her relationship to superiors—the board—and who presents an optimistic, glowing story of successful service delivery. Privately, though, directors are somewhat dissatisfied with their careers and the clients they serve. They can be characterized as Niskanen utility maximizing individuals well established in bureaucratic careers. Indeed, the most robust finding indicates that long-tenured bureaucrats have less trouble securing funding than new agency directors who have not been on the job as long.[6] In short, those who survive are fit at the Niskanen game. In the interest of career advancement, directors have evidently learned to live with cynicism and client disenchantment.

Perceptions and Goals: An Assessment of Community Services

Most social agencies offer a multitude of programs, often ranging from three to twenty-three. These organizations are thus, in practice, spread quite thin in a multidimensional service world. Some focus chiefly on designing and publicizing programs for social action and community change; others concentrate on the provision of specific services for individual clients on a one-to-one basis; yet others engage in overall planning on behalf of the entire community or corporate segments within. Although an exclusive focus on planning for or serving the elderly is the prerogative of a handful of agencies, many include one or more programs for senior citizens as part of their entire package of policies.

To evaluate community services we attempted two comparisons of response consistency based upon the respondents' assessment of agency priorities. First, does the respondents' perception of the agency's top priority reflect an internally consistent picture of priority as seen jointly by board members, directors, and staff workers? In ten of the nineteen agencies for which we completed multiple interviews, a consensus on first priority clearly prevailed. Yet for nine others, nearly half, no general agreement on top priority emerged. Thus, half of those agencies under investigation display no clear consensus on goal or program priority. Small wonder, then, that directors have a different view of serving clients than do staff workers, who must directly cope with client wants.

A second calculation sought to measure the overall perception of the content of the three priorities elicited during the interviews. The order of priority was here discounted as we sought only to identify similarity and difference in general content. Subjective views of agency functions present a more rosy picture as there appeared to be general consensus among the agency personnel in thirteen of the organizations: only six display a portrait of discord.

Eliminating staff replies disclosed that success with funding may depend on the director-sovereign relationship. In the nine instances where the director and board chairman agreed on content of priorities, seven directors report no problems with agency funding. In the five instances of disagreement, on the other hand, three directors suggest funding problems. (This result is, by Fisher's exact test, statistically significant.)

What inferences might we draw from this rather uncomplicated analysis? Simply this: if agency personnel do not have a clear understanding or agreement among themselves on the goals, purpose, and programs of their respective agencies, then how can a self-organized advocacy group of the elderly poor map an efficacious strategy to improve the quality of service delivery germane to their self-expressed wants? When a planning agency does not plan, when a legislating agency does not effectively legislate, and when a social change agency believes that it provides assistance with housing, then it seems unlikely that a group of elderly persons with limited education and other means will, even if effectively organized, knock on the correct door.

A recent study points precisely to a related problem.[7] The authors of this report compared the perceptions of priority service needs of public agency personnel with those of a sample of urban elderly poor. They found that services which are now currently offered (in a portion of Los Angeles County) may be lacking in relevance to the urban elderly poor. The older sample felt that values for relevance must include choice and individual acceptance, values not well supported by current services. The data show, according to the authors, that a chasm exists between what the urban elderly poor perceive as necessary in services and what the public agency representatives perceive as desirable. The proposed solution to this clash in perspectives is to insure that services begin to reflect desired life styles of the elderly poor, rather than an imposed, isolated set of bureaucratic, middle-class service values. Unless individual differences in wants and desires are permitted full expression, service programs will fall short of success in their purpose.

The interpretation of social agencies offered in this chapter sheds light on this clash in perspective. We have uncovered, we believe, a key reason why these perceptions differ: Niskanen bureaucrat maximizing behavior is not the same thing as client-pleasing behavior. To overcome this contradiction we propose, in the final chapter, some modifications in the present system of service delivery that should permit a more effective campaign to be waged on behalf of the urban elderly poor.

Who Decides for the Aged?
Implications for Policy

What began as a study of the urban elderly poor in a typical Model Cities community, strongly influenced by the contending views of leading gerontologists, has instead resulted in a characterization of the racial values and behavior of the elderly poor. Considerations of race supercede the factors inherent in chronological aging in determining the preferences of the elderly poor, their social action potential, and/or the likelihood that programs designed in their behalf can succeed. Although we set out initially to evaluate the social, psychological, physical, and political effects of aging among the urban elderly poor of all races, our attention quickly shifted to the profound differences that being white or black engenders among the elderly.

Old people are steadily growing in absolute numbers and as a relative percentage of the American population. Moreover, as the life expectancy of blacks increases, and as poor aged whites are forced to seek inexpensive inner-city accommodations, the problems of aging will increasingly be centered in the inner city where financial circumstances force blacks and whites into impoverished integrated neighborhoods. The one group of the aged who most require special assistance—the urban elderly poor—are thus the subjects of this book. Knowledge gleaned about the aged Model Cities' residents in Rochester is quite plausibly typical of the general conditions in which old poor people live. This detailed case study yields broad societywide implications, in terms of both descriptive understanding and prescriptive intervention.

We set out to build upon the work of many scholars who represent the professions of sociology, political science, social welfare, geron-tology, and economics, among others. Beginning with the notion that *needs* of human beings can only be correctly revealed from the *subjective,* personal standpoint of each individual, we constructed a research design that would not impose an external (middle-class) conception of basic needs upon the subjects of our investigation; we instead encouraged each of the elderly to express his or her own personal preferences on a number of different dimensions: the sociological—the family, social organizations, religion, friendship; the political—levels of political knowledge, awareness, participation, or interest in collective action; the psychological and physical—ease of mobility, degree of alienation, withdrawal, anxiety. The literature that a variety of professional disciplines has developed guided the preparation and pre-testing of an interview schedule, which would be used to understand the urban elderly poor—the purpose of our research. We now recapitulate the major findings.

Major Findings

1. Two worlds of aging exist side by side in Model Cities. This derives from the fact that to be old and black is substantially different from being old and white. The wants, values, and behavior of the urban elderly poor are more readily understood in terms of racial differences rather than distinctions in chronological age. Briefly, few blacks over seventy-five live in the inner city, a fact that reflects both perhaps a lower life expectancy and most certainly a recent history of northern migration; whites have held more satisfactory jobs; white average income significantly exceeds that of the average black household; whites are, on balance, better educated; white families suffer fewer divorces or separations; whites are long-time neighborhood residents whereas blacks are relative new-comers; whites are homeowners while the majority of blacks rents. To repeat, whites are richer, better educated, live longer, own their own homes, have better jobs, retain more stable households, are more established in the neighborhood, and are independent of welfare. Blacks, conversely, are poorer, live in less satisfactory accommodation (invariably rented), are poorly educated, are partially dependent on welfare, and are recently arrived in the area.

2. To our surprise, the expressed level of *need* is minimal. Most whites express values of self-reliance—they profess little interest in consuming welfare and other social services. Those most in *need* are old blacks, who, at anywhere from two to eight times the rate of whites, report having difficulties or shortages of basic urban amenities. But even for these problem areas that traditional gerontology investigates, the majority of blacks do not state a personal deficiency in transportation, meals, medical care, visiting of

friends, or the quality of their accommodations. Inner-city whites and blacks thus see and accept life on entirely different standards from the middle-class scholars who write books and articles about them.

3. Although elderly whites hold to a more positive general view of human nature than elderly blacks, immediate proximity to and increased interaction with blacks intensifies the already unfavorable images they project onto blacks. Whereas old blacks express a willingness to join whites in collective action to solve common problems of the elderly, the converse is not true. Old whites are not predisposed toward interracial cooperation. They resist the idea of integrated clubs, integrated employment, or multiracial social action. Black interest in multiracial pursuits is much more consistent with the favorable portrait of whites they project.

4. Most of the elderly poor show little interest in politics, possess rather limited information and, apart from voting, generally abstain from political activity. The black and well-educated are somewhat more knowledgeable and prone to participate, but the overall prospects for concerted multiracial action among the elderly poor appear dim.

5. Chronological age does not, as the literature had led us to expect, correlate with the psychological, social, and political aspects of advancing age; it is useful only as a predictor of reduced physical mobility. Reduced mobility, however, does not predict social, psychological, or political disengagement among the urban elderly poor. The disengagement thesis of aging is probably inapplicable to urban America in general inhabited by growing numbers of poor old whites and blacks.

Implications

By allowing each citizen to express his personal, subjective social wants, i.e., preferences, we arrive at our first and perhaps most important result. As to the *white* elderly poor, they are clearly saying: (1) leave us alone; (2) we are self-reliant and neither need nor want your help; (3) the last two decades have brought about the evolution of an environment in which it is no longer safe to live. We want, in short, the restoration of our neighborhood and way of life to mirror that of an era long since past, when it was safe to walk the streets at night. We do not like black people. We do not want to mix with them in social or political action groups. Our psychological well-being and desire for elementary security surpass any concern over meals, transportation, medical care, and its accompanying bureaucratic politics of service delivery. Indeed, in our view, the conversion of our formerly safe neighborhood into a sea of turbulence and physical insecurity is partly attributable to the prior efforts of those who do not have to live here, who can return to the suburbs every night.

Elderly *blacks* transmit a different message. In general, they admire white people, are genuinely enthusiastic about joining with whites in common programs, but express a greater measure of material want. Perhaps some means can and should to found to satisfy those wants. Assume our results typify the general condition of the urban elderly poor. Given the small likelihood for successful aged self-advocacy, how can these people find satisfaction of their wants?

1. Service delivery in Model Cities-type areas is characterized as often being monopolistic and generally paternalistic. Moreover, social service agents often have a different conception of client wants than do the clients themselves. Recall that the majority of elderly whites is not seeking assistance: even in the circumstance of a deteriorating materialistic life style, they continue to profess the norm of self-reliance under which they fashioned their productive years. Indeed, many who consume services have *no needs,* and many with needs do not consume the designated services.[1] Only those few whites who desire help and the *needy* old blacks are likely to benefit from an extension of the present system and they are a *distinct minority* among the elderly poor. An increase in conventional service delivery will not necessarily aid those with expressed social wants.

2. Given that the only correct determination of preferences is subjective, then the sole legitimate form of external assistance is one that aids those who subjectively determine they want assistance. The critical element in any assistance scheme must therefore be its market research aspects: to locate and identify the needy, to elicit their wants, and to supply the means for satisfying those wants.

Adoption of this strategy may at first appear to threaten established agencies. But, in fact, it should enable them to deliver to their clients what the clients really want. Confidence with service provision will rise both among the public and the clients, and funding bodies will have the satisfaction of knowing that genuine client wants are met. Administrators of these programs will therefore be directing highly valued and positively viewed programs. We do know that there is a group, albeit a minority of the elderly poor, who do want social services and whom the public is willing to help, if these programs are useful to the clients. But transportation need not be provided for those who prefer to stay at home, or meals to those who insist on preparing their own food, or clinic-based medical care to those who dislike public clinics. It is thus a nontrivial problem to locate those with genuine wants and to insure that correct identification of those wants is obtained if effective programs for aid to the elderly are to be implemented. We should not continue broadside services for those clients who do not want them. Not only are they given services they do not desire, but those who want help—and whom members of the public want to help—are crowded out of limited resources.

3. In our view, the potentially most rewarding way to assist many of the elderly poor is to give them increased cash, a desire expressed by many old persons during our community interviews. It is now clear that a large portion of the elderly population are poor because they lack money, not because they lack social services. The answer is to supply them with money, not with social services. This approach, cash supplements or a negative tax, constitutes an important alternative to the notion that coordination of and an increase in the supply of services are the answers to satisfying the needs of the elderly poor.

One major obstacle to this solution is found in the agencies themselves. For years we have observed that well-meaning agencies have defined the "needs" of the elderly and other clients in terms that agencies deem correct. This often results in client paternalism to insure that budgets are exhausted each year and the continued need for the program demonstrated despite what the clients may truly "need."[2]

Cash transfers or supplements to the poor permit each individual to seek and obtain the services he or she wants in an open market, in an environment as close to his or her own liking as possible. We thus concur with several policy options put forth in a recent paper.[3] These options call for decentralized market supply of services to be paid for in cash that has been provided by the government to the elderly poor. Both public and private agencies would compete for these funds by providing the kinds of services the elderly truly want.

Thus the elderly poor would be able to consume precisely those services they value. This is a market approach to planning and delivering services to the elderly, one that provides legitimate options or *choices* to consumers of all human services. Agency or program survival should depend largely on the number of satisfied customers, not on a director's political ability to appear successful to his superiors. In this way, agencies would receive money only for services to persons actually served.

There remains one residual category of elderly poor who would still require external supervision: the institutionalized, the physically incompetent, and those who possess little or no information about available options. It is to this group that the efforts of existing agencies should be directed. Other elderly poor can and should be given the option to exercise their own choices in pursuit of satisfying their own wants.

Appendixes

Appendix A
Community Survey
Interview Schedule

1971 CPC SURVEY
MODEL NEIGHBORHOOD AREA

NAME_____ CASE NUMBER _____

ADDRESS _____

CONFIDENTIAL

INTERVIEWER: "I'm   from the Citizen's
Planning Council. We're getting together some information that will help in the
organization of services for older adults. In order to do this, we need to
interview persons who are 55 years old or older. According to my information,
you are 55 or older. Is this correct?

"We're planning to interview about 500 people. We will put that information
into a report. Your name will not be used in any of the reports and will be kept
strictly confidential."

TIME INTERVIEW BEGAN: _____

DATE: _____

TRACT NUMBER: _____

BLOCK NUMBER: _____

(ENTER FIRST NAMES OF HOUSEHOLD OR FAMILY MEMBERS AND RECORD THE FOLLOWING INFORMATION FOR EACH. IF MORE THAN SIX PEOPLE LIVE IN THIS FAMILY, CODE THE INFORMATION ON THE NEXT PAGE.)

	RESPONDENT	ALL OTHER FAMILY MEMBERS

NAME

1. Relation to Head of Household (CHECK)

   Head
   Spouse
   Child
   Mother of Head
   Father of Head
   Parent-in-law
   Other Relative
   Friend or Boarder

2. Age (WRITE IN YEARS)

3. Sex (M or F)

4. Ethnic Group

   White
   Black
   Puerto Rican
   Other (SPECIFY)

5. National Background

   Italian
   Polish
   Irish
   British
   German
   African
   Ukranian
   Other (SPECIFY)
   No Answer

6. Religious Preference

Catholic
Protestant
Jewish
Other (SPECIFY)
None

7. Educational Level
Achieved (YEARS)

8. Technical (Job)

Training (SPECIFY KIND
AND AMOUNT)

9. Marital Status

Single
Married
Divorced
Separated
Widowed
Common Law

10. Employment Status

Employed full-time
Employed part-time
Student or pre-school
Housewife
Not Employed

11a. Where works

11b. Name of Job

11c. (IF PERSON INTERVIEWED IS NOT EMPLOYED OR IS A HOUSE-WIFE.)

(1) When did you last work? _____

(2) What kind of work did you do on your last job? _____

_____

(3) Was your last job full-time or part-time?   1. full-time
    2. part-time

(4) Why did you leave your last job?

1. retired
2. laid off
3. quit
4. health (SPECIFY)

_____
_____
_____

5. other (SPECIFY)

_____
_____
_____

(5) Are you looking for work at the present time?
(INCLUDING NEW KINDS OF WORK)

0. No
1. Yes

IF YES:

(1) What kind of work would you like to do? _____
_____

IF NO:

Why not?
(MARK THE SINGLE MOST IMPORTANT AN-
SWER. DO NOT READ THE ANSWERS.)

1. past retirement age
2. lack training
3. health
4. transportation
   difficulties
5. no jobs available
6. other (SPECIFY)

_____
_____

12. How long have you lived in this house? (YEARS) _____

13. Where did you live before? _____
_____

14. Where were you born?
(IF BORN OUTSIDE OF ROCHESTER), WHERE DID YOU LIVE BE-
FORE COMING TO ROCHESTER? _____

15. When were you born? _____

16. Is your neighborhood mostly
(READ A FEW)

    1. All White
    2. Mostly White
    3. About half White and half non-White
    4. All non-White

17. Are your friends
(READ A FEW)

    0. All White
    1. Mostly White
    2. All Black
    3. Mostly Black
    4. All Puerto Rican
    5. Mostly Puerto Rican
    6. Mixed Black-Puerto Rican
    7. Mixed White-Puerto Rican
    8. Mixed White-Black
    9. Mixed White-Black-Puerto Rican

18. Do you own your own home or do you rent?

    1. Own
    2. Rent
    3. Other (SPECIFY)

IF OWN:

    1. What do you say your house is worth today?

    1. 0-$4,999
    2. $5,000-$7,499
    3. $7,500-$9,999
    4. $10,000-$12,499
    5. $12,500-$14,999
    6. $15,000-$17,499
    7. $17,500-$19,999
    8. $20,000-$24,999
    9. over $25,000

IF RENTING

    1. What is your monthly rent?.

    1. less than $40
    2. $40-$69
    3. $70-$99

4. $100-$129
5. $130-$159
6. $160-$189
7. $190-$210
8. over $210

2. Does this include gas, light, heat and water?   0. Yes
                                                     1. No

19. Do you have a phone?   0. Yes
                                                     1. No

20. Are you happy with your house?   0. Unhappy
                                                     1. Happy

    IF UNHAPPY:

    1. Why are you unhappy with your house?
       (GIVE THE ONE IMPORTANT REASON TO YOU)

    _____

    _____

    _____

21. Are you happy with your neighborhood   0. Unhappy
                                                     1. Happy

    IF UNHAPPY:

    1. Why are you unhappy with your neighborhood?

    _____

22. If you had your choice, in what part of Rochester would you most like to
    live? (INCLUDING SUBURBS).

    _____

    _____

    People have different ways of thinking about problems faced by younger
    and older people. We'd like to know your way of thinking on some of these
    problems.

23a. Do you think most people care about helping other people?   0. Yes
                                                                  1. No

23b. Why do you think this way?

    _____

    _____

24a. As you have become older, what things are you interested in now? (And Why?)

_____

_____

24b. What things are you less interested in now? (And Why?)

_____

_____

_____

25a. Looking back, what do you think are the most pleasant things that happened to you in your life? (And Why?)

_____

_____

25b. What were the least pleasant? (And Why?)

_____

_____

26a. Do you feel people should take care of themselves all through life?   0. No
                                             1. Yes

26b. Why do you feel this way?

_____

_____

27a. Do you think people have fewer cares after they
retire?   0. No
                                             1. Yes

28. _Some people say_ that older people should retire to make room for younger people (for example, from jobs, or organizations, or politics). What do you think?

_____

_____

29a. Do you think older people should have their
own activities?   0. No
                                             1. Yes

29b. Why do you think this way?

_____

_____

30a. Do you think older people should mix with younger people?

    0. No
    1. Yes

30b. Why do you feel this way?

_____

_____

31. Do you think older people share the same kinds of problems among themselves?

    0. No
    1. Yes

32. Do you think older people can solve their common problems by working together?

    0. No
    1. Yes

33a. Do you think the retirement years are special years?

    0. No
    1. Yes

33b. Why do you think this way?

_____

_____

Now let's turn to some other information.

34. Would you mind letting me know what the total income of your family is from all sources? Just give me the letter off the card which matches your total family income.

    (WRITE DOWN MONTHLY OR YEARLY INCOME)

35. Do you have any close family who do not live with you?
(OTHER THAN THE ONES LISTED ON THE FIRST PAGE).

    0. No
    1. Yes

IF YES

(1) Who are they? (RELATIONSHIPS TO THE RESPONDENT)

_____

(2) Which ones live in the Rochester area? (SPECIFY)

_____

36a. How often do you visit with your family?
(INCLUDING RELATIVES) (HAVE RESPON-
DENT INDICATE WHICH SPECIFIC RELA-
TIVES)

1. Daily
2. Weekly
3. Monthly
4. Twice a year
5. Once a year

36b. Are there times you would like to visit with your family, but do not?

0. No
1. Yes

IF YES

(1) Why not?

_____

37. Do you belong to any social clubs or community organizations such as church groups, veterans groups, lodges, or settlement houses?

0. No
1. Yes

IF YES:

(1) Which groups do you belong to? (LIST UP TO THREE)

_____

_____

(2) Do you hold any offices or titles in any of these clubs?

0. No
1. Yes

(3) How often do you attend meetings?

1. Almost every time
2. Occasionally
3. Seldom
4. Never

38. How often do you attend religious services?
(DO NOT READ THE CATEGORIES)

1. Once or more times a day
2. Twice or more often per week
3. Once a week
4. Once or twice a month
5. Two or three times a year

6. On very special
occasions
7. Never

39a. How often do you get together with the friends
or neighbors you are closest with? . .

1. At least once a week
2. A few times a month
3. About once a month
4. A few times a year
5. Almost never

39b. Is it enough or would you like to get together
more often?

0. Enough
1. Not enough

IF NOT ENOUGH:

(1) Why not?

_____

40. Do you do any volunteer work at the present
time? (Volunteer work is work without pay for
some social agency, church or hospital)

0. No
1. Yes

IF YES:

(1) What are these activities? (LIST UP TO TWO ACTIVITIES)

_____

_____

IF NO:

(1) Would you be interested in volunteer work?

0. No
1. Yes

IF YES:

(1) What kind of volunteer work?
(DO NOT READ CATEGORIES)

1. Hospital
2. Social agency
3. Schools
4. Nursery
5. Area Clean-up
6. Other (SPECIFY)

_____

_____

41a. Would you say your health is usually

1. Excellent
2. Good
3. Fair
4. Poor

41b. Do you think there are times you should have seen a doctor, but did not?

0. No
1. Yes

IF YES: ←

(1) What is the most important things that kept you from going to the doctor?

1. Cost
2. Transportation
3. Difficulty with appointments
4. Location
5. Dissatisfaction with previous service
6. Other (SPECIFY)

_____

41c. Do you have any specific physical or health problems at the present?

0. Yes
1. No

IF YES: ←

(1) What are these problems? (LIST UP TO THREE PROBLEMS)

_____

_____

41d. Who do you see *most often* when you are ill? (MARK THE SINGLE MOST OFTEN. DO NOT READ THE CATEGORIES.)

1. Family doctor
2. Emergency Clinic
3. Druggist
4. Neighborhood Health Clinic
5. Hospital Clinic other than emergency
6. Other (SPECIFY)

_____

_____

42a. Do you have any problems getting meals?

    0. No
    1. Yes

IF YES:

    (1) What is your greatest problem?

    1. High cost
    2. Inadequate facilities
    3. Physically difficult
    4. Special diet problems
    5. Other (SPECIFY)

_____

42b. How do you usually get your meals?

    1. self or spouse
    2. other household
       members
    3. meals on wheels
    4. restaurants
    5. other (SPECIFY)

_____

43a. What do you generally use for getting around town (for other than work, for example, shopping or recreation)?
(READ A FEW)

    1. Walk
    2. Bus
    3. Taxi
    4. Family car
    5. Relatives car
    6. Friends car
    7. Other (SPECIFY)

_____

43b. Is getting around (transportation) a problem for you (for other than work, for example, for shopping or recreation)?

    0. No
    1. Yes

IF YES:

    (1) Why?

_____

_____

44a. What do you think is the biggest problem in your neighborhood?

44b. In what way is this a problem:

_____

45a. What do you think is the *biggest* problem in facing the people of Rochester today?

_____

45b. In what way is this a problem?

_____

46a. And how about the United States? What do you think is the most important problem facing the United States today?

_____

46b. In what way is this a problem?

_____

47. What are the most important problems you feel that government should concern itself with? (LIST UP TO TWO)

_____

_____

48. Where do you go when you have a personal problem? (What problem is this?)

_____

49. We would like to know something about what you do every day, and how hard or easy it is doing some things. As I read off some activities, please tell me if they are easy or hard to do, or if you can't do them at all.

(a) Going up and down stairs
1. Easy
2. Hard
3. Can't do it

(b) Go shopping
1. Easy
2. Hard
3. Can't do it

(c) Leave the building
1. Easy
2. Hard
3. Can't do it

(d) Walk around the room
1. Easy
2. Hard
3. Can't do it

(e)   Get into and out of bed

1. Easy
2. Hard
3. Can't do it

We'd like to ask your opinion on a number of political questions. Tell me if you agree or disagree with each statement.

50a. It isn't so important to vote when you know your party doesn't have a chance to win.

0. No
1. Yes

50b. A good many local elections aren't important enough to bother with.

0. No
1. Yes

50c. So many other people vote in the national election that it doesn't matter much to me whether I vote or not.

0. No
1. Yes

50d. If a person doesn't care how an election comes out, he shouldn't vote in it.

0. No
1. Yes

51a. I don't think public officials care about what people my age think.

0. No
1. Yes

51b. The way people vote is the main thing that decides how things are run in this country.

0. No
1. Yes

51c. Voting is the only way that people my age can have any say about how the government runs things.

0. No
1. Yes

51d. People my age don't have any say about what the government does.

0. No
1. Yes

51e. Sometimes politics and government seem so complicated that a person my age can't really understand what's going on.

0. No
1. Yes

52.   Some people say that citizens your age are not usually involved enough in politics. Why do you think some people your age are not involved in politics?

_____

_____

53.   What would make public officials listen to older citizens? (DO NOT READ THESE CATEGORIES)

1. Organize neighborhood groups
2. Demonstrate and riot
3. Letters to newspapers, televisions and radios

4. Working with govern-
ment programs for
example Model Cities

5. Other (SPECIFY)

_____

6. Nothing

54a. In talking with people about elections we find   0. No
that a lot of people aren't able to vote because   1. Yes
they aren't registered or were sick or just don't
have the time. How about you, did you vote in
the 1970 elections?

54b. Did you give any money, or buy tickets or   0. No
anything, to help the campaign for one of the   1. Yes
parties or candidates?

54c. Did you go to any political meetings, rallies,   0. No
dinners, or things like that?   1. Yes

54d. Did you do any work for one of the parties or   0. No
candidates?   1. Yes

54e. Did you talk to any people to try to show them   0. No
why they should vote for one of the parties or   1. Yes
candidates?

55a. What is your favorite part of the newspaper?

_____

55b. What is your favorite television program?

_____

56. We are trying to find out what influence different kinds of people and
organizations make on the public. Here is the list of people who have been
in the news recently. Do you know who they are? I will read off a list of
names. Please tell me who they are.

a.   Richard Nixon _____

b.   George Wallace _____

c.   F.I.G.H.T. _____

d.   Wyoma Best _____

e.   Stephen May _____

f.   Kermit Hill _____

g. Spiro Agnew _____

h. Model Cities _____

i. A.B.C. (Action for A Better Community) _____

57a. Which political party do you feel closest to?

(IF RESPONDENT IDENTIFIES HIMSELF AS AN INDEPENDENT ASK:)

(1) Which of the parties do you feel closest to? _____

57b. Have you always supported the same party? _____ 0. No
                                                                    1. Yes

IF NO:

(1) When did you change? _____

(2) From what party did you change? _____

(3) Do you remember why you changed? _____

We would like to ask your feelings on some governmental and community matters.

58a. Do you feel the government is handling the   0. No
problems of older citizens well?   1. Yes

58b. Do you feel younger people in the community   0. No
understand older people and their problems?   1. Yes

58c. Do you feel older people should have a definite 0. No
say in the running of the government?   1. Yes

58d. Do you feel private agencies (such as settlement 0. No
houses, hospitals and social agencies) are hand- 1. Yes
ling the problems of older citizens well?

59a. Do you feel Governor Rockefeller is handling his 0. No
job well?   1. Yes

59b. Do you feel President Nixon is handling his job 0. No
well?   1. Yes

59c. Who did you vote for in the 1968 election for 0. Nixon
President?   1. Humphrey
                                                  2. Wallace
                                                  3. No Answer
                                                  4. Did not vote

59d. Who did you vote for in the 1970 election for Senator?

    0. Buckley
    1. Goodell
    2. Ottinger
    3. No Answer
    4. Did not vote

59e. Who did you vote for in the 1970 election for Governor?

    0. Rockefeller
    1. Goldberg
    2. No Answer
    3. Did not vote

59f. If an election for President of the United States were being held today, who would you vote for if the three candidates were Humphrey, Nixon and Wallace?

    0. Humphrey
    1. Nixon
    2. Wallace
    3. No Answer

59g. If the three candidates were Muskie, Nixon, and Wallace, for whom would you vote for President of the United States?

    0. Muskie
    1. Nixon
    2. Wallace
    3. No Answer

IF WHITE, CONTINUE WITH THE NEXT PINK PAGE [Page 108].

IF BLACK, JUMP TO THE GREEN PAGE [Page 109].

IF PUERTO RICAN, JUMP TO THE WHITE PAGE [Page 110].

* * *

(PINK PAGE)

WHITES ONLY

These days there is a lot of talk about how Blacks and Whites feel about each other. We would like your feelings about this issue.

60a. Some say that Blacks have been trying to get ahead too fast. Others feel that they haven't gotten ahead enough. How about you? Do you feel that Blacks are trying to get ahead too fast, are they going too slowly, or are they moving about the right speed?

1. Too fast
2. Too slowly
3. About right

I am going to describe some situations to you and I want to know your own feelings. Tell me if you would like it or not.

60b. If you are working now and you had to work on the same job with Blacks?

0. Not like it
1. Like it

IF DID NOT LIKE IT:

(1) Why not?

_____

60c. If Blacks belonged to the same clubs and organizations with you?

0. Not like it
1. Like it

IF DID NOT LIKE IT:

(1) Why not?

_____

60d. If a club or organization for older people were formed in your neighborhood and Blacks belonged?

0. Not like it
1. Like it

IF DID NOT LIKE IT:

(1) Why not?

_____

60e. What about a community action group of older citizens? If one were formed in your neighborhood, would you be interested in joining it? (A Community action group is a group that gets together to solve common problems.)

0. Would not be interested
1. Would be interested

NOW GO TO THE NEXT PAGE   OMIT THE GREEN PAGE.

(GREEN PAGE)

BLACKS ONLY

These days there is a lot of talk about how Blacks and Whites feel about each other. We would like your feelings about this issue.

61a. Some say that Blacks have been trying to get ahead too fast. Others feel that they haven't gotten ahead enough. How about you? Do you feel that Blacks are trying to get ahead too fast, are they going too slowly, or are they moving about the right speed?

    1. Too fast
    2. Too slowly
    3. About right

61b. Some people say political parties should have members from all races. Some say that each racial group should be represented by their own parties. What do you think?

    1. Multi-racial parties
    2. Each race has its own party

I am going to describe some situations to you and I want to know your own feelings. Tell me if you would like it or not.

61c. If you were working now and you had to work on the same job with Whites?

    0. Not like it
    1. Like it

IF DID NOT LIKE IT:

(1) Why not?

_____

61d. If Whites belonged to the same clubs and organizations with you?

    1. Not like it
    2. Like it

IF DID NOT LIKE IT:

(1) Why not?

_____

61e. If a club or organization for older people were formed and whites belonged to it also?

    0. Not like it
    1. Like it

IF DID NOT LIKE IT:

(1) Why not?

_____

61f. What about a community action group of older citizens? If one were formed in your neighborhood, would you be interested in joining it? (A Community action group is a group that gets together to solve common problems.)

    0. Would not be interested
    1. Would be interested

NOW GO TO THE NEXT PAGE   *ALL* RESPONDENTS

ALL RESPONDENTS AGAIN

(ASK EACH RESPONDENT. ASK FOR BOTH RACES)

	WHITES	BLACKS
62a. Ambition. Do you think most Whites try to get ahead? How about Blacks?	1. High 2. Low 3. Neither	1. High 2. Low 3. Neither
62b. Intelligence. Do you think most Whites are smart? How about Blacks?	1. High 2. Low 3. Neither	1. High 2. Low 3. Neither
62c. Honesty. Do you think most Whites tell the truth? How about Blacks?	1. High 2. Low 3. Neither	1. High 2. Low 3. Neither
62d. Cleanliness. Do you think most Whites are clean? How about Blacks?	1. High 2. Low 3. Neither	1. High 2. Low 3. Neither
62e. Responsibility. Can you trust Whites to do what they say they will do? How about Blacks?	1. High 2. Low 3. Neither	1. High 2. Low 3. Neither

63. Are you happy with the success of the Red Wings?

1. Yes
2. No
3. No Answer
4. Don't know

PRESENT CERTIFICATE

THANK RESPONDENT

* * *

INTERVIEWER'S PAGE

1. Time interview completed _____

2. Total length of interview _____

3. Was the interview private, that is, just the respondent and the interviewer, or were there other people present?

   1. Private interview
   2. Others present
      (FILL IN NUMBER)

   IF OTHERS PRESENT:

   (1) Did they listen or did they take part in the interview?

   1. Just listened
   2. Took part in the interview

   (2) Did they help with the answers?

   1. No
   2. Yes

4. Was the respondent

   1. Confined to bed
   2. Confined to a wheel-chair
   3. Blind (or extremely poor eyesight)
   4. Very hard of hearing
   5. Other (SPECIFY)

   _____

5. Language used in the interview

   1. English
   2. Spanish
   3. Italian
   4. Other (SPECIFY)

   _____

6a. Respondent's attitude at the beginning of the interview

   1. Very interested
   2. Interested
   3. Not very interested
   4. Antagonistic
   5. Nervous, uncertain

6b. Respondent's attitude at the end of the interview.

   1. No change
   2. More interested, helpful
   3. Less interested, helpful
   4. Hurrying to get it over
   5. Other

   _____

7. Any other comments? Use this space to write any and all comments you think will be helpful.

8. Interviewer's signature _____

Appendix B
Agency Survey Interview Schedule

CITIZENS PLANNING COUNCIL OF ROCHESTER AND MONROE COUNTY, INC.

70 North Water Street · Rochester, New York 14604 · Area Code 716 454-2770

Dear

The Social Research unit of the Citizens Planning Council is currently engaged in an Administration on Aging research project. The purpose of this project is to gain a better understanding of how community agencies figure in the lives of older persons and others in the Rochester area.

Because of your vantage point as an agency director we would greatly appreciate an interview with you. We will similarly be interviewing other community agency directors, staff members, and board members.

The interview will take about one hour. This is in no way an evaluation of your agency's program. Your responses will be seen only by the project research staff and will be held in strict confidence.

We would also appreciate your help in recommending an agency board member and staff person whom we could interview.

An interviewer will call you in the near future and if agreeable to you, schedule an interview at your convenience.

Sincerely yours,

Richard S. Sterne, Ph.D.
Director of Social Research

RSS/cd

July 14, 1972   *CITIZENS PLANNING COUNCIL*

AoA Survey

Community Agency
Interview

Purpose of Interview (to be explained by interviewer, ad lib)

Note: letter previously sent out requesting permission for interview.

I appreciate your giving about one hour of your time today to help us in our study on the aging.

The purpose of the study is to gain a better understanding of the way in which community agencies figure in the lives of older persons to other persons in the Rochester area.

I am interviewing you, other agency executives, staff members, and board members because of the unique vantage point you have professionally in the community.

Your responses will be seen only by the project research staff and will be held in strictest confidence. They will not be shared verbally with anyone associated with your or any other agency.

After the study, the findings will be made available to you in the form of statistical summaries, with no individual responses identifiable. I would, therefore, encourage your candor and spontaneous responses.

NAME: _____

AGENCY: _____

POSITION: _____

DATE: _____

1. Much has been said recently in both professional and lay circles about the wants of the older person (55 or older). From your vantage point as _____ what do you see as the *three* most important wants facing the older person?

   (1)

   (2)

   (3)

2. You mentioned _____ (select first "want" listed). In what specific way do you think this effects the older person?

3. How successfully do you see these wants currently being met within the Rochester community:

   Successfully _____   Somewhat unsuccessfully _____

   Somewhat successfully _____   Unsuccessfully _____

   Explore: What do you think the reason is for this?

4. In general, how responsive do you think the Rochester community is to the wants of the older persons?

   Responsive _____   Somewhat unresponsive _____

   Somewhat responsive _____   Unresponsive _____

   Explore:

5. What particular influence do you think the Rochester Model Cities Neighborhood area has on the daily life of the older resident?

6. How would you rank in order of priority your agency's service goals?

   First _____

   Second _____

   Third _____

7. I would like to ask you about some characteristics of the majority of clients your agency serves:

116

a. In what areas of Rochester do most of them live?

_____

b. In what portions of the Model Neighborhood Area (MNA) are they concentrated?

_____

c. What is their age range?

(If age range in MNA differs, specify)

d. What proportion is now working?

e. What kind of jobs do most of them hold when they work?

_____

(If jobs in MNA differ, specify)

f. What, do you estimate, is the median family income of your clients?

_____

(Distinguish clients not working and those who are working) (If incomes in MNA differ, specify.)

g. What proportion of your clients are:

Black _____

White _____

Puerto Rican _____

Other _____

(If proportions in MNA differ, specify)

h. What are their main national backgrounds?

_____

(If backgrounds in MNA differ, specify)

8. Generally, how readily do you think the older person in this neighborhood seeks help for his needs?

Readily _____   Not too readily _____

Somewhat readily _____   Not well at all _____

9. How informed do you think the older person in your agency's neighborhood is about the services you offer?

Informed _____   Somewhat informed _____

Somewhat informed _____   Uninformed _____

10. How often do older residents seek help or service from your agency regardless of whether you are able to provide that help?

Frequently _____   Occasionally _____

Fairly often _____   Never _____

11. What types of services do they request?

12. Are you able to meet these requests? Yes _____ No _____

If *yes*, which ones?

13. How often do relatives or friends of an older person seek out your agency's services for them?

Frequently _____   Occasionally _____

Fairly often _____   Never _____

14. What types of services do they request?

15. Are you able to meet these requests? Yes _____ No _____

If *yes*, which ones?

16. Of the services you are currently not able to provide, are any being considered for future programs?

Yes _____   No _____

If *yes*, which ones?

Explore "No":

17. What are the major drawbacks to providing these services currently?

    Explore:

18. How much of an indirect effect do you think your agency has on the life of the older residents in the MNA?

    Great deal _____   Not very much _____

    Somewhat _____   None _____

    Explore if other than "none":

19. How often do you make referrals to other community agencies for services requested by an older person but not available at your agency?

    Frequently _____   Occasionally _____

    Fairly often _____   Never _____

20. What agencies do you refer to most often?

21. Does your agency use older persons as volunteers? Yes _____ No _____

    If yes, in what capacities?

    If no, why are they not used?

22. If you were to develop an idea for a new program for a specific client group, to whom would you turn first?

    Explore: board, staff, style, etc.

23. How receptive is the neighborhood or this community to program changes?

    Receptive _____   Somewhat unreceptive _____

    Somewhat receptive _____   Unreceptive _____

24. How receptive is the agency board to program changes?

    Receptive _____   Somewhat unrecptive _____

    Somewhat receptive _____   Unreceptive _____

Explore: *Board member–agency relationships*

25. How receptive is the staff to program change?

    Receptive _____   Somewhat unreceptive _____

    Somewhat receptive _____   Unreceptive _____

26. How receptive are the clients to program changes?

    Receptive _____   Somewhat unreceptive _____

    Somewhat receptive _____   Unreceptive _____

27. How could the people of this neighborhood (Model Cities Area) be most helpful in implementing new program requests?

28. How could the agency board be most helpful in implementing new program requests?

    Explore: What do you think the board member in general sees as his role in the agency

29. In starting new programs cooperation is often needed from other agencies or groups. In your agency, who usually has the task of fostering cooperative working relationships?

30. What is the most successful method you have found for fostering such cooperative relationships?

    Explore:

31. Do you think the board would support you on a proposal to add/add more services for the aging?

    Yes _____   No _____

    If "No", why not?

32. How do you think the staff would react to (adding/adding more) services for the aging?

Favorably _____   Somewhat unfavorably _____

Somewhat favorably _____   Unfavorably _____

Explore:

33. Much has been said lately about consumers putting pressure on businesses and on health and social service agencies. Have any groups approached your agency with specific requests or demands?

    Yes _____   No _____

    If "*Yes*," what *groups*?

    Explore: group compositions, nature of requests, etc.:

34. How do you handle this type of situation?

35 and 36 – Executives Only

35. As *agency executive*, what approach do you find to be most successful in working with the staff?

    Explore:

36. As *agency executive*, what approach do you find to be most successful in working with the board?

    Explore:

37. When you wish to alter key aspects of your agency's operation, what are some major problems you generally confront?

    Explore:

38. Would you care to comment on any programs you have particularly wanted to see started in the Model Cities neighborhood but have not come about?

    Yes _____   No _____

    If "Yes," explore: age group, problem focus, etc.

    If "No," go on to #41

39. What agency/agencies could best administer or implement this/these program(s)?

40. Based on your experience, what steps or techniques would you use to influence the community to start such a program?

41. In your opinion, do you think a staff member should act so as to meet the needs of a client even if a particular act differs from explicitly stated agency policies?

    Yes _____   No _____

    Explore: (MAY REQUIRE AN EXAMPLE)

42. Different people in social agencies have differing target groups. If you could predict your agency's future, what services or client groups would you say it would focus on?

    Explore: for example

    Same as now _____

    Continue present program plus _____

    Cut back _____

    Cut back _____ and add _____

43. Is this future direction a major interest you also share professionally so far as your career interests go?

    Yes _____   No _____

    If "No," what other directions do you see for your professional interests?

44. As an (agency director/staff member/board member) what from your earlier experience has been most helpful in your current activities with this agency?

45. How satisfied are you with social services in general as a field in which to work when you compare it with other types of work which might appeal to you?

Satisfied _____   Somewhat dissatisfied _____

Somewhat satisfied _____   Dissatisfied _____

46. How satisfied are you working with the types of wants presented by the clients who currently come to your agency?

Satisfied _____   Somewhat dissatisfied _____

Somewhat satisfied _____   Dissatisfied _____

47. How satisfied are you with this particular agency as a place with which to be associated/work, when you compare it with other agencies of this type?

Satisfied _____   Somewhat dissatisfied _____

Somewhat satisfied _____   Dissatisfied _____

Explore: dissatisfactions

48. How satisfied are you with the working relationship (of) (you have with your) colleagues within this agency?

Satisfied _____   Somewhat dissatisfied _____

Somewhat satisfied _____   Dissatisfied _____

Explore:

49. How satisfied are you with the working relationships (you have with colleagues in) other social agencies in the community?

Satisfied _____   Somewhat dissatisfied _____

Somewhat satisfied _____   Dissatisfied _____

Explore:

50. How satisfied are you with the agency policies when you consider the agency clients and the problems they present for your services?

Satisfied _____   Somewhat dissatisfied _____

Somewhat satisfied _____   Dissatisfied _____

Explore: Who has responsibility for developing agency policies?

51. How satisfied are you with the *board members'* understanding of the day-to-day particulars involved in carrying out the agency goals?

Satisfied _____   Somewhat dissatisfied _____

Somewhat satisfied _____   Dissatisfied _____

Explore:

52. How satisfied are you with the *staff members'* understanding of the day-to-day particulars involved in carrying out the agency's goals?

Satisfied _____   Somewhat dissatisfied _____

Somewhat satisfied _____   Dissatisfied _____

Explore:

53. How satisfied are you with the *clients' understanding* of the day-to-day particulars involved in carrying out the agency goals?

Satisfied _____   Somewhat dissatisfied _____

Somewhat satisfied _____   Dissatisfied _____

Explore:

54 omit for executive interviews

54. How satisfied are you with the *executive's understanding* of the day-to-day particulars involved in carrying out the agency goals?

Satisfied _____   Somewhat dissatisfied _____

Somewhat satisfied _____   Dissatisfied _____

Explore:

55. From your experience as an agency director, what approaches would you say are best for organizing and implementing services for older persons?

* * *

INTERVIEWER'S PAGE

1. Be sure responses to all questions are filled in before returning the interview schedule. The completed schedule is your report on an interview.

2. Replay tape (if used). Review it to record any pertinent content not already included on schedule.

3. Summarize on the schedule form all pertinent data from open-ended and exploratory questions. Include both content and observational data, e.g., interviewer's affect, style of response, etc.

   Also complete the following information:

4. Condition of interview (circle):
   1. Private
   2. Others present (who?)

5. Interviewee's attitude at beginning of interview:
   1. Very interested
   2. Interested
   3. Not very interested
   4. Antagonistic
   5. Nervous, uncertain

6. Interviewee's attitude at the end of the interview:
   1. No change
   2. More interested, helpful
   3. Less interested, helpful
   4. Hurrying to get it over
   5. Other

   _____

7. Other comments. Use this space to write any comments you think will be helpful.

8. Time Interview began: _____

   Time Interview ended: _____

   Length of interview: _____

9. Interviewer's Signature _____

Appendix C
List of Interviewed Agencies

1. Action for a Better Community
2. Baden Street Settlement House
3. Citizens Planning Council
4. Community Chest
5. Department of Social Services
6. F.I.G.H.T.
7. Genesee Settlement House
8. Housing Council of Monroe County
9. Ibero-American Action League
10. Metro Act
11. Model Cities
12. Monroe County Council on Aging
13. Neighborhood Health Center & Rochester Health Network
14. New Life Council
15. Northeast Property Upgrading Association
16. Office of Human Development
17. Rochester Management
18. Senior Citizens Action Council
19. Senior Citizens of Monroe County (Model Cities)
20. Urban Development Corporation
21. Urban League
22. Visiting Nurse Service

Appendix D
Agency Regressions

This appendix presents the multiple regression results on which a portion of the discussion in Chapter 8 is based. In the following table, several different regressions are presented which, in effect, test for the Niskanen effect. Each column represents a regression with a different dependent variable. The independent variables should be interpreted as follows:

PUBPRIV: An ordinal variable indicating the degree to which the respondent's agency is privately funded.

SOVEREIGN: the number of funding sources for the respondent's agency.

DIR: a dummy variable indicating if the respondent is the director of an agency.

LEVEL: an ordinal variable indicating the respondent's level in the agency, e.g., member of staff.

BLACK: a dummy variable indicating if respondent is black.

NTIME: Time, in years, that respondent has been with agency.

NAGEA: Age, in years, of agency.

Table D-1
Niskanen Effect in Agencies (N=60)

	Board Cooperative?	Board Receptive to Program Change	Satisfied with Board Understanding?	Board not design new Programs?	Board Hostile to Funding New Programs?	Cooperative with Other Agencies?
PUB PRIV	-.28*	-.29*	-.41*	-.23	-.20	-.04
SOVEREIGN	-.08	-.16	-.18	.36*	25	-.26
DIR	-.29*†	-.25*†	-.27*†	.29*†	.14	-.33*†
LEVEL	-.00	.23†	.09	.09	.27*†	-.03
BLACK	-.17	-.03	-.20	-.10	.01	-.16
NTIME	-.28*	-.11	21	-.25	-.03	.01
NAGEA	.09	.08	.13	-.06	-.41*†	-.04
R^2	.24	.25	.34	.20	25	.21

Notes: 1. Entries are standardized beta coefficients.
2. * indicates significance at .05 level.
3. † indicates items discussed in Chapter 8.

Notes

Notes for Introduction

1. *Developments in Aging 1970. A Report of the Special Committee on Aging, United States Senate. Report No. 92-46.* (Washington, D.C.: U.S. Government Printing Office, 1971), p. 126.

Notes for Chapter 1

1. These data are taken from Robert J. Havighurst, Chairman, "Research and Development Goals in Social Gerontology," *Gerontologist* 9, 4 (Winter 1969, Part II): 5-6.

2. Mary L. Brooks Lambing, "Social Class Living Patterns of Retired Negroes," *Gerontologist* 12, 3 (Autumn 1972, Part I): 285.

3. Elaine Cumming and William E. Henry, *Growing Old* (New York: Basic Books, 1961).

4. Marjorie Fiske Lowenthal and Deetje Boler, "Voluntary vs. Involuntary Social Withdrawal," *Journal of Gerontology* 20, 3 (July 1965): 363-371.

5. Edward G. Ludwig and Robert L. Eichhorn, "Age and Disillusionment: A Study of Value Changes Associated with Aging," *Journal of Gerontology* 22, 1 (January 1967): 59-64.

6. Margot Tallmer and Bernard Kutner, "Disengagement and the Stresses of Aging," *Journal of Gerontology* 24, 1 (January 1969): 70-75.

7. Thomas L. Tissue, "Disengagement Potential: Replication and Use as an Explanatory Variable," *Journal of Gerontology* 26, 1 (January 1971): 76-80.

8. Gordon F. Streib and Clement J. Schneider, S.J., *Retirement in American Society, Impact and Process* (Ithaca and London: Cornell University Press, 1971), especially pp. 171-180.

9. Ibid., p. 180.

10. The following works could be said to represent the "activity" theory perspective: E.W. Burgess, "Social Relations, Activities, and Personal Adjustment," *American Journal of Sociology* 59, 4 (Janu-

ary 1954): 352-360; R.J. Havighurst and R. Albrecht, *Older People* (New York: Longmans, Green, 1953); B. Kutner, D. Fanshel, A. Togo, and S.W. Langner, *Five Hundred over Sixty* (New York: Russell Sage Foundation, 1956); D. Lebo, "Some Factors Said to Make for Happiness in Old Age," *Journal of Clinical Psychology* 9, 4 (October 1953): 384-390; S. Reichard, F. Livson, and P.G. Peterson, *Aging and Personality* (New York: John Wiley, 1962); M. Tallmer and B. Kutner, "Disengagement and Morale," *Gerontologist* 10, 4 (Winter 1970, Part I): 317-320; and S.S. Tobin and B.L. Neigarten, "Life Satisfaction and Social Interaction in the Aging," *Journal of Gerontology* 16, 4 (October 1961): 344-346. See also Aaron Lipman and Richard S. Sterne, "Aging in the United States: Ascription of a Terminal Sick Role," *Sociology and Social Research* 53, 2 (January 1969): 194-203, for a parallel discussion.

11. Bruce W. Lemon, Vern L. Bengston, and James A. Peterson, "An Exploration of the Activity Theory of Aging: Activity Types and Life Satisfaction among In-Movers to a Retirement Community," *Journal of Gerontology* 27, 4 (October 1972): 511-523.

12. Ibid., p. 519.

13. One recent paper notes the failure of both the "activity" and "disengagement" theories to explain documented instances that contradict what would have been expected from either or both of the theories. In their place, the author proposes a new socio-environmental theory of aging built around the interrelationship of two conceptual components: (1) environmental effects such as homogeneity, residential proximity, and local protectiveness; and (2) personal resources influencing behavior flexibility such as health, solvency, and education. The specific results of the application of this framework to a study of criminal victimization in old age is, for our purposes, less important than noting his observation on the absence of a general framework governing the study of aging among gerontologists. See Jaber F. Gubrium, "Toward a Socio-Environmental Theory of Aging," *Gerontologist* 11, 3 (Autumn 1971, Part I): 281-284.

14. Abraham Holtzman, *The Townsend Movement: A Political Study* (New York: Bookman Associates, Inc., 1963).

15. Frank A. Pinner, Paul Jacobs, and Philip Selznick, *Old Age and Political Behavior* (Berkeley and Los Angeles: University of California Press, 1959).

16. See, for example, Frank A. Pinner, "Theories of Political Participation and Age," in Wilma Donahue and Clark Tibbits (eds.), *Politics of Age* (Ann Arbor: University of Michigan Press, 1962), pp. 63-74 and Angus Campbell, "Social and Psychological Determinants of Voting Behavior," in Donahue and Tibbits, pp. 87-100.

17. "The Aging and Aged Blacks," *1971 White House Conference on Aging* (Washington, D.C.: U.S. Government Printing Office), p. 3.

18. Irving Rosow, *Social Integration of the Aged* (New York: Free Press, 1967), p. 1.

Notes for Chapter 2

1. For an historical account of the region designated as Model Cities in Rochester, see Blake McKelvey, "Rochester's Near Northeast," *Rochester History* 29, 2 (April 1967): 1-23.

2. This discussion is excerpted from Robert E. Gamer, *The Politics of Urban Development in Singapore* (Ithaca and London: Cornell University Press, 1972), p. 193.

3. *Developments in Aging 1970. A Report of the Special Committee on Aging, United States Senate. Report No. 92-46.* (Washington, D.C.: U.S. Government Printing Office, 1971), pp. 126-127.

4. See Richard S. Sterne and Roger M. Weir, *Needs of the Elderly in the Model Cities Area, Rochester, New York* (Rochester: Citizens Planning Council of Rochester and Monroe County, Inc., 1970). (mimeo)

5. Richard S. Sterne, *Social and Health Services in the Model Cities Area, Rochester, New York* (Rochester: Council of Social Agencies of Rochester and Monroe County, Inc., 1969), p. II-3. (mimeo)

6. We do not intend here to support the Moynihan argument on the "deterioration" of black families. For a full debate see Lee Rainwater and William L. Yancey, *The Moynihan Report and the Politics of Controversy* (Cambridge: M.I.T. Press, 1967). Many feel that the analyses in the original "Moynihan Report" were inadequate, that one can discern different types of black families when

income and region are taken into account. Andrew Billingsley notes that 75 percent of black families, on a nationwide basis, are not broken and that in the upper income levels, 90 percent are intact. He warns against single-factor hypotheses in discussing black problems. See *Black Families in White America* (Englewood Cliffs, N.J.: Prentice-Hall, 1968), pp. 197-215.

There has been much argument that the enumeration of black households itself has been faulty, causing an only *apparently* higher rate of broken homes among blacks. See, for example, Richard S. Sterne and Ruth Owens Kruse, "The Missing Male—The Missing School Child in the Slums: a Correlation?" *Education and Urban Society* 1, 1 (November 1968): 81-92.

The use of highly trained indigenous black and white interviewers, the careful quality controls exercised in our work, and the high rate of sample completion give us confidence that the data reported herein are accurate. Thus we extrapolate from the observed differences between blacks and whites only to conclude that different types of family structure predominate among old black and white residents within Model Cities, and that these differences may affect, on balance, their outlooks and wants.

Notes for Chapter 3

1. See, for example, Stephen J. Cutler, "The Availability of Personal Transportation, Residential Location, and Life Satisfaction Among the Aged," *Journal of Gerontology* 27, 3 (July 1972): 383-389; Bruce W. Lemon, Vern L. Bengston, and James A. Peterson, "An Exploration of the Activity Theory of Aging: Activity Types and Life Satisfaction among In-Movers to a Retirement Community," *Journal of Gerontology* 27, 4 (October 1972): 511-523; and David L. Adams, "Correlates of Satisfaction Among the Elderly," *Gerontologist* 11, 4 (Winter 1971, Part II): 64-68.

2. For a related case study of this point, see Richard S. Sterne, Alvin Rabushka, and Helen A. Scott, "Serving the Elderly?—An Illustration of the Niskanen Effect," *Public Choice* 13 (Fall 1972): 81-90.

3. Richard S. Sterne, *Social and Health Services in the Model Cities Area, Rochester, New York* (Rochester, N.Y.: Council of Social Agencies, 1969), p. II-17. (mimeo)

Notes for Chapter 4

1. J.S. Furnivall, *Netherlands India* (Cambridge: The University Press, 1939), p. 446.

2. See, for example, Irving Rosow, *Social Integration of the Aged* (New York: The Free Press, 1967).

3. See Richard S. Sterne and Roger M. Weir, *Needs of the Elderly in the Model Cities Area, Rochester, New York* (Rochester: Citizens Planning Council of Rochester and Monroe County, Inc., 1970), p. 78. (mimeo)

4. See Alvin Rabushka, *Race and Politics in Urban Malaya* (Stanford: Hoover Institution Press, 1973), pp. 63-67.

Notes for Chapter 5

1. For an excellent summary of this literature see Matilda White Riley and Anne Foner, *Aging and Society. Volume One: An Inventory of Research Findings* (New York: Russell Sage Foundation, 1968), pp. 463-482.

2. See, for example, Martin Fishbein (ed.), *Readings in Attitude Theory and Measurement* (New York: John Wiley, 1967).

3. For an interesting and provocative account of the overall futility of the model cities program in general, see Roland L. Warren, "The Model Cities Program: Assumptions—Experience—Implications," mimeo, paper presented at the National Conference on Social Welfare, Dallas, Texas, May 17, 1971.

4. "Interest-Group Liberalism and the Politics of Aging," *Gerontologist* 12, 3 (Autumn 1972, Part I): 267.

Notes for Chapter 6

1. Elaine Cumming and William E. Henry, *Growing Old* (New York: Basic Books, 1961).

2. Though we examine disengagement with our survey data, it should be pointed out that cross-sectional data generally provide information on the age structure of society but do not directly disclose how individuals age. Only life-cycle analyses (longitudinal

data) trace genuine shifts in the same individual over time. Differences among aging categories should not be directly construed as the result of individual aging. For an excellent discussion on this point see Matilda White Riley and Anne Foner, *Aging and Society. Volume One: An Inventory of Research Findings* (New York: Russell Sage Foundation, 1968), pp. 7-8. In this study of the elderly poor in Rochester's Model Cities, though, we believe that persons presently aged fifty-five to sixty have substantially similar upbringings to those aged seventy to seventy-five. We therefore believe that an examination of the survey data is a reasonable empirical test of disengagement. See the discussion that follows in the text.

3. Crudely put, factor analysis examines the intercorrelations among a group of variables and can be made to suggest a number of "underlying" statistical factors or dimensions each of which seems to explain the behavior of a different subset of the original variables. The chief benefit of this exercise is to reduce the magnitude of the analytical problem; rather than having to deal with some sixty-odd individual variables, one can argue that several clusters of them seem to be interrelated enough so that each cluster can be treated as a single variable.

Factor analysis might, therefore, appear to be an invaluable asset to the practitioners of a primitive science who have the use of elegant new computing machinery to apply to an abundant supply of data, but have precious little theory to guide them in such an application. For our purposes, though, both a logical investigation and contingency analysis have cast doubt upon the viability of the "disengagement" concept. The factor analysis only comprised a last-ditch effort to insure that no dimension of aging, which might explain social attitudes or behavior, had eluded our inquiry. Since the analysis yielded nothing new, but only confirmed our prior findings, we do not display the factors and their loadings. Anyone interested in the full set of survey data should write to the authors. For an excellent discussion of the pitfalls of factor analysis see John E. Mueller, *Approaches to Measurement in International Relations* (New York: Appleton-Century-Crofts, 1969), pp. 309-311.

4. Gisela V. Labouvie, "Implications of Geropsychological Theories for Intervention: The Challenge for the Seventies," *Gerontologist* 13, 1 (Spring 1973): 13.

5. K. Warner Schaie, "Reflections on Papers by Looft, Peterson,

and Sparks: Intervention Toward an Ageless Society?" *Gerontologist* 13, 1 (Spring 1973): 32.

Notes for Chapter 7

1. Jack Leff, *Advocacy in the Field of Aging* (New York: National Council on Aging, 1972).

2. In order to obtain information on any previous efforts made to organize the urban elderly poor for social or political advocacy we placed advertisements in both Senior Opportunities and Services Technical Assistance Bulletin (Published for the Office of Economic Opportunity, Volume 2, Number 12, November/December 1972) and the Older Worker Specialist Newsletter (NCOA's Institute of Industrial Gerontology, Volume 1, Number 2, November/December 1972).

We received replies from such cities as Philadelphia and Tucson including another confidential report of how a successfully (though externally assisted) organized group, which had effectively brought about an increase in services for the elderly in its locale, was ultimately stifled when existing agency domains appeared threatened. On balance, our search disclosed that each of the elderly poor organized groups depended on the support of professionals or others who were not themselves poor. Also, an examination of other elderly groups in Model Cities indicated their dependence on professional direction or other external assistance.

3. Joel D. Aberbach and Jack L. Walker, *Race in the City* (Boston: Little, Brown, 1972), pp. 98-99.

Notes for Chapter 8

1. The title of this chapter is taken from a previous essay. See Richard S. Sterne, Alvin Rabushka, and Helen A. Scott, "Serving the Elderly?—An Illustration of the Niskanen Effect," *Public Choice* 13 (Fall 1972): 81-90.

2. William A. Niskanen, Jr., *Bureaucracy and Representative Government* (Chicago and New York: Aldine-Atherton, 1971), pp. 3-9.

3. In addition to Niskanen's book, see also Gordon Tullock, *The Politics of Bureacracy* (Washington, D.C.: Public Affairs Press, 1965) and Anthony Downs, *Inside Bureaucracy* (Boston: Little, Brown, 1967).

4. Niskanen, *Bureaucracy,* p. 23.

5. See Gordon Tullock, "Information Without Profit," *Papers on Non-Market Decision Making* (1966): 141-160.

6. See "Serving the Elderly?" in which we obtained a similar result. In a study of a low cost meals program for the elderly in Miami we discovered that the more successful service centers were the older centers—where staff members had been on the job longer than elsewhere.

7. Mark J. Riesenfeld, Robert J. Newcomer, Paul V. Berlant, and William A. Dempsey, "Perceptions of Public Service Needs: The Urban Elderly and the Public Agency," *Gerontologist* 12, 2 (Summer 1972, Part I): 185-190.

Notes for Chapter 9

1. Elsewhere we present an interesting case study of this point based upon an investigation of old people in Miami, Florida. See Richard S. Sterne, Alvin Rabushka, and Helen A. Scott, "Serving the Elderly?—An Illustration of the Niskanen Effect," *Public Choice* 13 (Fall 1972): 81-90.

2. See, for example, William A. Niskanen, Jr., *Bureaucracy and Representative Government* (Chicago and New York: Aldine-Atherton, 1971).

3. Bernard Greenblatt and Theodore Ernst, "The Title III Program: Field Impressions and Policy Options," *Gerontologist* 12, 2 (Summer 1972, Part I): 191-196.

Bibliography

Books

Aberbach, Joel D. and Jack L. Walker. *Race in the City*. Boston: Little, Brown, 1972.

Cumming, Elaine and William E. Henry. *Growing Old*. New York: Basic Books, 1961.

Donahue, Wilma and Clark Tibbits (eds.). *Politics of Age*. Ann Arbor: University of Michigan Press, 1962.

Downs, Anthony, *Inside Bureaucracy*. Boston: Little, Brown, 1967.

Fishbein, Martin (ed.). *Readings in Attitude Theory and Measurement*. New York: John Wiley, 1967.

Furnivall, J.S. *Netherlands India*. Cambridge: The University Press, 1939.

Havighurst, Robert J. and R. Albrecht. *Older People*. New York: Longmans, Green, 1953.

Holtzman, Abraham. *The Townsend Movement: A Political Study*. New York: Bookman Associates, Inc., 1963.

Kutner, Bernard, D. Fanshel, A. Togo, and S.W. Langner. *Five Hundred over Sixty*. New York: Russell Sage Foundation, 1956.

Leff, Jack. *Advocacy in the Field of Aging*. New York: National Council on Aging, 1972.

Niskanen, William A., Jr. *Bureaucracy and Representative Government*. Chicago and New York: Aldine-Atherton, 1971.

Pinner, Frank A., Paul Jacobs, and Philip Selznick. *Old Age and Political Behavior*. Berkeley and Los Angeles: University of California Press, 1959.

Rabushka, Alvin. *Race and Politics in Urban Malaya*. Stanford: Hoover Institution Press, 1973.

Rainwater, Lee and William L. Yancey. *The Moynihan Report and the Politics of Controversy*. Cambridge: M.I.T. Press, 1967.

Reichard, S., F. Livson, and P.G. Peterson. *Aging and Personality*. New York: John Wiley, 1962.

Riley, Matilda White and Anne Foner. *Aging and Society*. Volume

One: An Inventory of Research Findings. New York: Russell Sage Foundation, 1968.

Rosow, Irving. *Social Integration of the Aged.* New York: Free Press, 1967.

Simpson, Ida Harper and John C. McKinney (eds.). *Social Aspects of Aging.* Durham, N.C.: Duke University Press, 1966.

Streib, Gordon F. and Clement J. Schneider, S.J. *Retirement in American Society, Impact and Process.* Ithaca and London: Cornell University Press, 1971.

Tullock, Gordon. *The Politics of Bureaucracy.* Washington, D.C.: Public Affairs Press, 1965.

Periodicals

Adams, David L. "Correlates of Satisfaction Among the Elderly." *Gerontologist* 11, 4 (Winter 1971, Part II): 64-68.

Binstock, Robert. "Interest-Group Liberalism and the Politics of Aging." *Gerontologist* 12, 3 (Autumn 1972, Part I): 265-280.

Burgess, E.W. "Social Relations, Activities, and Personal Adjustment." *American Journal of Sociology* 59, 4 (January 1954): 352-360.

Clark, Margaret. "Patterns of Aging Among the Elderly Poor of the Inner City." *Gerontologist* 11, 1 (Spring 1971, Part II): 58-66.

Cutler, Stephen J. "The Availability of Personal Transportation, Residential Location, and Life Satisfaction Among the Aged." *Journal of Gerontology* 27, 3 (July 1972): 383-389.

Cutler, Stephen J. "Voluntary Assocation Participation and Life Satisfaction: A Cautionary Research Note." *Journal of Gerontology* 28, 1 (January 1973): 96-100.

Greenblatt, Bernard and Theodore Ernst. "The Title III Program: Field Impressions and Policy Options." *Gerontologist* 12, 2 (Summer 1972, Part I): 191-196.

Gubrium, Jaber F. "Toward a Socio-Environmental Theory of Aging." *Gerontologist* 11, 3 (Autumn 1971, Part I): 281-284.

Gubrium, Jaber F. "Continuity in Social Support, Political Interest, and Voting in Old Age." *Gerontologist* 12, 4 (Winter 1972): 421-423.

Havighurst, Robert J. "Research and Development Goals in Social Gerontology." *Gerontologist* 9, 4 (Winter 1969, Part II): 5-9.

Jackson, Jacquelyne Johnson. "Negro Aged: Toward Needed Research in Social Gerontology." *Gerontologist* 11, 1 (Spring 1971, Part II): 52-57.

Jackson, Jacquelyne Johnson. "Social Impacts of Housing Relocation upon Urban, Low-Income Black Aged." *Gerontologist* 12, 1 (Spring 1972): 32-37.

Kent, Donald P. "The Elderly in Minority Groups: Variant Patterns of Aging." *Gerontologist* 11, 1 (Spring 1971, Part II): 26-29.

Labouvie, Gisela V. "Implications of Geropsychological Theories for Intervention: The Challenge for the Seventies." *Gerontologist* 13, 1 (Spring 1973): 10-14.

Lambing, Mary L. Brooks. "Social Class Living Patterns of Retired Negroes." *Gerontologist* 12, 3 (Autumn 1972, Part I): 285-288.

Lambing, Mary L. Brooks. "Leisure-Time Pursuits Among Retired Blacks by Social Status." *Gerontologist* 12, 4 (Winter 1972): 363-367.

Lebo, D. "Some Factors Said to Make for Happiness in Old Age." *Journal of Clinical Psychology* 9, 4 (October 1953): 385-387.

Lemon, Bruce W., Vern L. Bengston, and James A. Peterson. "An Exploration of the Activity Theory of Aging: Activity Types and Life Satisfaction Among In-Movers to a Retirement Community." *Journal of Gerontology* 27, 4 (October 1972): 511-523.

Lipman, Aaron and Richard S. Sterne. "Aging in the United States: Ascription of a Terminal Sick Role." *Sociology and Social Research* 53, 2 (January 1969); 194-203.

Ludwig, Edward G. and Robert L. Eichhorn. "Age and Disillusionment: A Study of Value Changes Associated with Aging." *Journal of Gerontology* 22, 1 (January 1967): 59-64.

Lowenthal, Marjorie Fiske and Deetje Boler. "Voluntary vs. Involuntary Social Withdrawal." *Journal of Gerontology* 20, 3 (July 1965): 363-371.

McKelvey, Blake. "Rochester's Near Northeast." *Rochester History* 29, 2 (April 1967): 1-23.

Riesenfeld, Mark J., Robert J. Newcomer, Paul V. Berlant, and William A. Dempsey. "Perceptions of Public Service Needs: The

Urban Elderly and the Public Agency." *Gerontologist* 12, 2 (Summer 1972, Part I): 185-190.

Schaie, K. Warner. "Reflections on Papers by Looft, Peterson, and Sparks: Intervention Toward an Ageless Society?" *Gerontologist* 13, 1 (Spring 1973): 31-35.

Sterne, Richard S. and Ruth Owens Kruse. "The Missing Male—The Missing School Child in the Slums: a Correlation?" *Education and Urban Society* 1, 1 (November 1968): 81-92.

Sterne, Richard S., Alvin Rabushka, and Helen A. Scott. "Serving the Elderly?—An Illustration of the Niskanen Effect." *Public Choice* 13 (Fall 1972): 81-90.

Tallmer, Margot and Bernard Kutner. "Disengagement and the Stresses of Aging." *Journal of Gerontology* 24, 1 (January 1969): 70-75.

Tallmer, Margot and Bernard Kutner. "Disengagement and Morale." *Gerontologist* 10, 4 (Winter 1970, Part I): 317-320.

Thune, Jeanne M., Celia R. Webb, and Leland E. Thune. "Interracial Attitudes of Younger and Older Adults in a Biracial Population." *Gerontologist* 11, 4 (Winter 1971, Part I): 305-310.

Tissue, Thomas L. "A Guttman Scale of Disengagement Potential." *Journal of Gerontology* 23, 4 (October 1968): 513-516.

Tissue, Thomas L. "Disengagement Potential: Replication and Use as an Explanatory Variable." *Journal of Gerontology* 26, 1 (January 1971): 76-80.

Tobin, S.S. and B.L. Neigarten, "Life Satisfaction and Social Interaction in the Aging." *Journal of Gerontology* 16, 4 (October 1961): 344-346.

Tullock, Gordon. "Information Without Profit." *Papers on Non-Market Decision Making* (1966): 141-160.

Wells, Larry L. "Welfare Embarrassment." *Gerontologist* 12, 2 (Summer 1972, Part I): 197-200.

Official Reports

The Aging and Aged Blacks. 1971 White House Conference on Aging. Washington, D.C.: U.S. Government Printing Office, 1971.

Developments in Aging 1970. A Report of the Special Committee on Aging, United States Senate. Report No. 92-46. Washington, D.C.: U.S. Government Printing Office, 1971.

Sterne, Richard S. and Roger M. Weir. *Needs of the Elderly in the Model Cities Area, Rochester, New York.* Rochester: Citizens Planning Council of Rochester and Monroe County, Inc., 1970.

Sterne, Richard S. *Social Health Services in the Model Cities Area, Rochester, New York.* Rochester: Council of Social Agencies of Rochester and Monroe County, Inc., 1969.

Index

About the Authors

Richard S. Sterne is associate professor of urban studies and sociology at the University of Akron. He received the B.A. from Swarthmore College, the M.A. from Duke University, and the Ph.D. from the University of Pennsylvania. He has extensive experience in research and administration in gerontology, race relations, and welfare; he has taught at the University of Miami, the State University College at Geneseo, and St. John Fisher College. Dr. Sterne's publications and reviews have appeared in *Contemporary Sociology, Phylon, Public Choice, Sociology and Social Research, Urban Affairs Quarterly*, and other periodicals. He is the author of *Delinquent Conduct and Broken Homes.*

James E. Phillips received the B.A. from St. John Fisher College and has done graduate study in sociology at Rutgers University. He is a research analyst with the Probation Employment and Guidance Program in Rochester, New York, conducted by the Monroe County Adult Probation Department under a grant from the Law Enforcement Assistance Administration.

Alvin Rabushka is associate professor of political science at the University of Rochester. He is the author of *Race and Politics in Urban Malaya* (Hoover Institution Press, 1973), *The Changing Face of Hong Kong* (American Enterprise Institute for Public Policy Research, 1973), *A Theory of Racial Harmony* (University of South Carolina Press, 1973), and coauthor, with Kenneth A. Shepsle, of *Politics in Plural Societies* (Charles E. Merrill, 1972). He is presently preparing a study of policy-making and budgeting in the Hong Kong government.